INSTRUCTOR'S MANUAL

To Accompany

INTRODUCTION TO
SOCIOLOGY

FIFTH EDITION

By Henry L. Tischler

Prepared By

Patrick J. Ashton
Indiana University–Purdue University Fort Wayne
ashton@smtplink.ipfw.indiana.edu

HARCOURT BRACE COLLEGE PUBLISHERS

Fort Worth Philadelphia San Diego New York Orlando Austin San Antonio
Toronto Montreal London Sydney Tokyo

ISBN: 0-15-503127-9

Address editorial correspondence to:
Harcourt Brace College Publishers
301 Commerce Street, Suite 3700
Fort Worth, TX 76102

Address orders to:
Harcourt Brace & Company
Permissions Department
6277 Sea Harbor Drive
Orlando, FL 32887-6777
1-800-782-4479 or 1-800-433-0001 (in Florida)

Printed in the United States of America

5 6 7 8 9 0 1 2 3 4   023   9 8 7 6 5 4 3 2 1

TABLE OF CONTENTS

Chapter   **Page**

INTRODUCTION

TEACHING INTRODUCTORY SOCIOLOGY: PHILOSOPHICAL AND PEDAGOGICAL REFLECTIONS

It may seem somewhat unusual to begin an Instructor's Manual with a set of philosophical and pedagogical reflections. However, as I am the author of the in-text Study Guide and Practice Tests, the Part Openers for each section of the text, the co-author of "A Word to the Student: How to Get the Most Out of Sociology" at the front of the textbook, as well as the author of the Test Bank and this Instructor's Manual, I thought that it might be useful for you, the instructor of an introductory sociology course, to know something of the thinking that went into the making of this material. Further, as someone who has taught sociology to both traditional and non-traditional students for almost twenty years, I have some ideas about the process that I would like to share with you. It is, of course, not necessary for you to buy into any or all of this philosophy in order to find the ancillaries useful. I simply offer my ideas as part of a dialogue about teaching introductory sociology. I hope you find my ideas useful and/or provocative. I would like to hear from you so that we can make future editions even more useful.

Approaches to Teaching the Introductory Sociology Course

At most institutions, introductory sociology functions primarily as a service course. In other words, most of the students in this class are there because they *have* to be — that is, introductory sociology is a required general education course that, in most students' eyes, they must "get out of the way" in order to get to the really important and useful courses in their major. Or perhaps your course just happened to be offered at the right time and place to fit an empty slot in some students' schedules. Or maybe some students perceive that introductory sociology, because it is about "people," is a "gut" course that should guarantee a pretty good grade with a minimum of effort. After all, this isn't quantum physics or calculus or biochemistry or even a foreign language, is it?

Given these pre-existing attitudes, how should we approach the teaching of introductory sociology? Of course we want to convey to them the seriousness and importance of sociology as a discipline. And it wouldn't be too bad to recruit a few majors along the way, either. But how to do this? To my mind, introductory sociology should be a *skills* as well as a *survey* course. An introductory course in any discipline is, to a large extent, always a survey course. It aims to acquaint students with the concepts, theories, research findings, and approaches to knowledge that are relatively unique to that discipline. But what's interesting about sociology is that, because it's about society and social life, our discipline has the possibility of proving useful to students in the broadest possible context — within the classroom and the university as well as in their work, family, and community lives. If we can help students to develop the skills to *apply* sociology to their lives, then they will be far more effective in living those lives. But *what* skills should introductory sociology students be learning, and *how* should we help them to apply those skills? In this Introduction I will try to briefly address both of these questions.

The Purpose of the Introductory Sociology Course

I think that the most important skills that sociologically-informed students can possess are the skills necessary for understanding and coping effectively with social change. In an era of rapid social change, such skills are empowering. Students who possess accurate knowledge of how the social world works, and who

1

understand how to apply that knowledge are more likely as individuals to successfully cope with ongoing changes and, more importantly, as members of various communities, to be able to collectively affect the pace and direction of change. Of course there are no guarantees. Just knowing how and why things tend to happen the way that they do doesn't ensure that we can make them come out the way we want them to. There are too many variables, and the scale and scope of change are often too large. But, I tell my students, understanding the process gives us a much greater chance of successfully intervening in it than not having a clue as to what's going on and just randomly trying out strategies.

What does it mean to have the skills to understand and deal with the process of social change? In my syllabus (see the Appendix at the end of this Introduction) and in my first lecture I suggest that there are three interrelated sets of skills that students can — and should — develop in an introductory sociology course. These skills are as follows.

1. **Understanding and Comparing Goals.** It makes no sense to try to follow a roadmap if we don't know where we want to go. Having a goal or goals not only gives us a destination, but it also generates for us measures of how successful we are in moving toward it. Underlying and informing divergent sets of goals are differing sets of values leading to contrasting ideological perspectives. Introductory sociology must not, of course, tell students what their goals or values should be. But our courses can give students the skills to understand the social processes by which goals are generated, the social influences that shape differing sets of goals, the dynamics of conflict among different goals, and to decode and contrast the values and ideological perspectives underlying goals. With these skills, students should be more knowledgeable and effective both collectively and as individuals. (See the Resources section at the end of this Introduction for material to assist in this skill development.)

2. **Understanding Social Dynamics.** Once students have a better idea of where they want to go, and how and why other groups of people may have opposing goals, introductory sociology students must develop the skills to try to reach those desired goals. They must learn the "nuts and bolts" of how the social world works, and how to effectively intervene within it. Thus they must learn basic sociological concepts (norm, culture, status, etc.) and explore basic social processes (socialization over the life cycle, power, social change, etc.). In each case, knowledge must be tested by application to real-life situations. Along the way, students must acquire knowledge of research methods in order to answer with some confidence the question "How do we know that we know what we think we know?"

3. **Understanding the Pattern of Social Change.** Once students have a sense of where they want to go and the mechanisms by which they might get there, they need two more important skills: the ability to understand where society is now and where it seems to be going — that is, the pattern of social change. With this knowledge they can hopefully intervene to support those directions of change that are in agreement with their values and goals and oppose those that aren't. There is not time, of course, to cover all aspects of society and social change in one introductory sociology course. Therefore I focus on patterns of inequality by class, race, gender, and geography (cities vs. suburbs, developed vs. underdeveloped countries).

My entire introductory sociology course is then focused around giving students the information and the practice to develop these three skill areas. I think that you can easily fit all the topics in an introductory sociology textbook into these three categories. The advantage of packaging the topics this way is, first of all, it focuses student attention on something that they can plainly see is in their own self-interest and can benefit them in their lives outside of the classroom. Thus it is easier to generate enthusiasm for sociology in general and the introductory sociology course in particular. Secondly, by focusing the course on skill acquisition, the textbook becomes not just a collection of "facts," but a tool to inform, support, and assist in the development of these important skills. Students tend to read it with more of a purpose in mind.

Students do not come to us as "blank slates," of course. In general, they have at least 18 years of experience (and, in the case of many of my students, considerably more years than that!) interacting in society and social situations. The unique experiences and personal biographies that students bring to an introductory sociology course are not to be denigrated; in fact they are a valuable resource that can be drawn from and built upon in the course. On the other hand, it is true that many of the everyday "common sense" understandings that students have about the social world are frequently idiosyncratic, misperceived, and sometimes flat-out wrong. Thus we must encourage students to look at society and their lives within it in a fresh, open-minded way. This is the meaning of the statement in my syllabus that sociology is an unfamiliar way of looking at the familiar. We can use their experiences as the raw material of analysis, but we must develop the skills to see and analyze it in fresh ways.

If we give our introductory sociology students this kind of grounding in understanding and dealing with society and social change, I am convinced that we will make them better and more effective individuals and —more importantly — citizens. Along the way, we will be showing them the real value of sociology and a sociological understanding of the social world. Students just might be inspired to take another sociology course or even to consider becoming a major. Regardless of what students decide to do afterward, however, if we teach our introductory sociology course as primarily a way of developing practical intellectual skills we will have provided a truly useful and valuable service course.

USING THE BUILT-IN FEATURES OF THE TEXTBOOK

In order to acquire any sort of skills, people must be *active*. The "extras" that are built into Tischler's textbook are designed to encourage and assist students in actively acquiring the skills of sociological analysis and application. First, there is "A Word to the Student: How to Get the Most Out of Sociology" at the front of the textbook. I strongly encourage you to point it out to your students and remind them to take a look at it. Most students (and professors) don't read prefatory material in a textbook — often with good reason. However this preface, which is written specifically for students, contains valuable information on how to effectively read the textbook, function in class, study, and take tests successfully. This information is distilled from the latest research on developmental learning, and contains the same proven-effective skills that are taught in developmental learning centers and, these days, increasingly for profit in private learning centers and/or on videotape. Unless you draw students' attention to the material at the front of the textbook, however, they are likely to overlook it.

The basic message of our preface to the students (I co-wrote it with a developmental learning specialist) is that success in this and all other courses lies in becoming an active student. The built-in Study Guide (the colored-edge pages following each chapter of the textbook) is designed to implement this advice with regard to Tischler's textbook. It too is based on the latest developmental learning techniques. Each chapter's Study Guide begins with a set of learning objectives. Stated in behavioral terms, these objectives indicate what students should be able to *do* when they are finished studying and learning the material in the text chapter. You may want to indicate to students in your class which objectives you intend to emphasize. You may also want to make up your own objectives to fit your own approach to the subject matter. (See the Resources section at the end of this Introduction for books that can assist you in constructing behavioral objectives.) At any rate, knowing what they are expected to be able to do allows students to stay motivated and to measure and evaluate their own progress in learning the material.

In our preface to the textbook, students are advised to begin studying a textbook chapter by reflecting on what they already may know about the subject. This approach not only recognizes and validates the experiential knowledge each student brings to their introductory course, it encourages active engagement with the material from the start. A good place to begin this process is with the learning objectives. How much of this can students already do? What things do they want to know more about or be able to do better? Students

3

are then advised to read the chapter summary *before* reading the text. The summary should familiarize them with all the main points. They can then read to find, probe, and understand these main points. Cognizant of this approach, I tried to make sure that the chapter summaries in the Study Guide are comprehensive and detailed enough to make prereading worthwhile. The summaries are subdivided by the main chapter headings to facilitate organizing the ideas and connecting them back to the text. This form of organization also allows students to study more efficiently by identifying the parts of the chapter where they might need to focus more time and effort. In addition, every term or concept that is highlighted and defined in the text chapter is also highlighted and defined in the chapter summary. This way students are alerted, once again, to what will be important to their understanding of the material.

An important component of active reading, students are advised in the preface, is to ask questions and then read to find the answers to those questions. One technique taught by developmental learning specialists is to turn each bold-faced heading in the chapter into a question. You might want to explicitly encourage your students to perform this exercise because, if they do, they cannot fail to be actively engaged with the text. Another, even more important way for students to engage with the material is for them to complete the exercises in the Study Guide for each learning objective. The exercises are formatted in a workbook style that encourages students to organize, apply, and practice the material in an efficient manner. Students are often reluctant to write in their textbooks, either because of conditioning in elementary and secondary school or because they are afraid to damage the resale value of the text. You may want to point out to them that that was the point of making the text relatively inexpensive in the first place — to make it affordable for students to really use a book effectively by writing in it and not worrying about any significant financial consequences. Besides, I ask students, what is your education worth to you? What is the cost of a textbook relative to the price of the course itself? (An especially small ratio in the case of the relatively inexpensive Tischler text.) Given that by completing the exercises in writing you cannot *not* learn the material, how can you afford *not* to do them? The learning objective exercises are never a mere regurgitation of significant points from the text. Rather, students are asked to reflect on, evaluate, and, in many cases, apply the material for each learning objective. Instructors may want to use these exercises for in-class discussions, student writing assignments and projects, and/or essay exam questions. I encourage instructors to see these exercises only as a starting point, and to modify and elaborate on them in line with the purposes, style, and requirements of your particular course.

In an introductory sociology course, it is necessary for students to learn the definitions of important concepts, both as a matter of intellectual clarity and precision and as a means to facilitate proper and efficient application of these concepts in their lives. Thus the Study Guide contains a matching exercise involving every term that is highlighted and defined in the text and its definition or description. While the list of concepts is scrambled, the definitions are ordered to match the sequence in which the concepts appear in the text chapter. Answers are provided at the end of the Study Guide chapter. Again, in completing this exercise, the student must actively make connections. Likewise, if important theorists or researchers are mentioned in a text chapter, another matching exercise is provided to connect their names to the reason we should know about and remember them. These latter are generally kept to a minimum, as I feel that introductory sociology is not about names and dates, but about concepts that students can apply to their lives. Instructors may want to incorporate the matching exercises into exams; they do not appear as such in the Test Bank, as it is my personal opinion that matching exercises are not the best way to test knowledge or application of the concepts.

Next the Study Guide presents five or six Critical Thinking/Application Questions. These are generally much broader than the learning objective exercises and are less likely to have a "right answer." In order to construct a reasonable answer, however, students must really understand the sociological concepts on which the question is based. The questions are ordered from least to most difficult so that students can build confidence as they work through them. Again, you may find these questions useful for in-class discussions, student projects, or essay questions.

4

At the back of the book students will find a Practice Test for each chapter of the text. The tests consist of 40–50 true/false and multiple-choice questions. The questions are organized into sections by major topic heading. This makes the test more diagnostic — that is, by examining the percentage of right and wrong answers in each section, students can identify strengths and weaknesses and spend their study time more efficiently. Within each major section, the questions are *not* presented in the same order in which they are covered in the text — that is, the questions are scrambled. Research shows that students score about 3 percent higher when questions are presented in text order. Thus, scrambled questions may provide a truer test of knowledge. Answers to the practice tests are at the back of the textbook so students can check themselves. Furthermore, should you wish to reward or reinforce students who take the time to work through the practice tests, selected questions from these tests appear in the Test Bank. In each case, these questions (and some which repeat learning objective exercises) are identified as such, so that you can choose to use them, or not, as you see fit.

DESIGNING AN INTRODUCTORY SOCIOLOGY COURSE

Developing Goals and Objectives

The key principle in designing any course is to *start with the outcome in mind.* What do we want students to have accomplished by the end of the course? What will they be able to do that they couldn't do, or couldn't do as well, at the beginning of the course? This gives us our overall goals; the next step is to turn those goals into behavioral objectives. Listed in the Resources section at the end of this Introduction are some books that may help with this process. As far as the substance of those objectives goes, I have suggested one model above and in my sample syllabus. The American Sociological Association's Teaching Resource Center (address in the Resource section) has available syllabi sets and other materials that provide a broad range of other examples. If you or your department don't have at least the Introductory Sociology syllabi set, you should get it immediately. It is quite inexpensive and very valuable.

Writing a Syllabus

The syllabus you design and give to your students at the beginning of your course should be as detailed as possible. Besides goals and behavioral objectives, the syllabus should give students information about your pedagogical philosophy and style. In addition, I think that the syllabus is a form of contract; in it you state explicitly what you require of students and how they can expect to be evaluated and graded (which are not necessarily the same thing). All important policies should be spelled out here. When it comes to something as important as requirements, evaluation and grading, I don't think it's possible to give students too much information.

What should those requirements be, and how should they be evaluated? These questions cannot be answered here; the answers will vary by institution and by instructor background, outlook, and preference. I can say, however, that a principle that I try to implement in my courses is this: Have high standards and then do everything possible to help students meet those standards. It is not wrong, in my opinion, to require students to demonstrate that they actually know and can apply all (or at least most) of the important material. What is wrong is to establish this requirement without helping students to develop the skills and acquire the knowledge to meet it. Using this fifth edition of Tischler's text with all of the built-in skill-builders is certainly one way to advance this goal. Another way is to make sure that you always inform students of exactly what you expect them to know and do. For instance, in my introductory sociology course I provide students with a list of every important concept that they will need to know for the exam (see Appendix). Exam questions are drawn exclusively from this list. That way no time and effort are wasted trying to "psych out" the instructor and guess at what may be important. Coursework should not be a guessing game. If we think some things are worth learning, why not tell the students and then help them learn the material?

How much material should you cover? The obvious answer is "as much as possible." Given the constraints of time, however, you won't be able to cover everything. What compromises, then, are appropriate? My bias is to err on the side of depth more than that of breadth. To speak of "coverage" always reminds me of painting a wall. Working quickly with a good supply of paint we can "cover" a lot of wall space. But all we have done is apply a thin layer to the surface. And although the wall looks really nice immediately after being covered, when the paint wears off you have little trace left of the paint or the painter. "Coverage" leaves students with little in the future. On the other hand, if we get students interested, enthusiastic, and informed on a relatively small number of issues, they will have the motivation and the tools to investigate further. I'm not arguing to leave out important parts of a standard introduction to sociology; I'm only suggesting that we try not to err too much on the side of "coverage."

Requirements for Mastery Learning and Evaluation

Course requirements, I think, should be designed with two purposes in mind: (1) to facilitate active learning of important concepts, and (2) to allow students to demonstrate that they have mastered those concepts. There are, of course, many ways of accomplishing these tasks. In-class discussions, study groups, projects, and the textbook's built-in Study Guide and Practice Tests are just some of the ways that come to mind. Many of these same activities can be used to accomplish the second goal — that of evaluation. Individual and group presentations, oral exams, various kinds of writing projects, and, of course, tests are other possibilities. Testing — especially in large introductory courses — is perhaps the most widely used method of evaluation. Done properly, it can be much more than just a way of assigning grades. It can be a learning experience for students as well as a way for them to demonstrate mastery. A discussion of this philosophy can be found in the Introduction to the Test Bank. I would simply summarize that philosophy here by outlining the following principles of appropriate testing.

1. **Tests should cover important, nontrivial material.** Objective tests, in particular, often seem "mickeymouse" because they cover material that is easily put into objective questions instead of material that is really important. Essay tests can fall into a similar trap when they are unclear and encourage wild speculation rather than analysis, application, synthesis, or evaluation of important concepts.

2. **Tests should allow students to demonstrate mastery of important concepts.** To accomplish this goal, testmakers must provide challenging questions that test higher-level cognitive skills — that is, skills that go beyond mere recall of factual knowledge. Furthermore, tests should be designed in such a way that only students who really know the material can do well. This doesn't mean that students should be tricked (see next item); it only means that a variety of commonsensical —but wrong — options should be provided to eliminate (or at least reduce) the premium for good guessing.

3. **Tests should never attempt to fool or trick students.** There is no angrier confrontation between student and instructor than the one with the student who feels that she or he was tricked or deceived. In many cases the student has a legitimate grievance, in my opinion. There simply is no need to try to fool or trick students. It is not pedagogically — or personally — wise, or necessary. Although I realize there may be some difference of opinion, every attempt has been made to ensure that none of the questions in the Practice Tests or the Test Bank employs deception.

The Uses of Writing in Introductory Sociology Courses

In recent years, increasing attention has been focused on writing both as a means of learning and as a means of evaluation. This is a welcome development, in my opinion, especially in light of the changing nature of the college student body in most places. As we have known for some time now, the pool of young, white, middle-class college students is declining. In most urban universities, large percentages of students are 25 and older and/or part-time. And these institutions, as well as traditional liberal arts colleges, are looking to increase minority recruitment, fully cognizant of the fact that soon nearly 40 percent of the 18-24 year olds in this country will be Hispanic, African American, or Asian American.

One thing about this "new majority" of non-traditional college students is that they tend to be less well-prepared for college. They often lack basic writing and communication skills or, if they have them, they are more intimidated by the institutional structure of the university and less confident of expressing themselves. To a great degree, I would contend, this is due to the fact that the traditional white middle-class subculture of the university is more foreign to them. It is thus our responsibility as educators to address ourselves to the anxieties and concerns of the new majority students — to help them "find their voices" — without alienating or disenfranchising more traditional students in the classroom.

At the same time, many college educators are coming to recognize the importance of writing as pedagogy. In part, of course, this reflects the aforementioned skill deficits that have drawn so much attention. But the very need to teach so many students remedial writing and communication skills has begged the question of why this is important, and opened up a healthy — in my view — discussion on the role of writing throughout the curriculum.

As many of our colleagues in English departments have been trying to tell us for some time now, and some of us have known, or are just starting to learn, writing for and in college classes is neither a product nor a purely technical skill; rather, it is a non-linear, recursive process. Of course we sociologists have always asserted that language, as symbolic communication, is shaped by its cultural context. Words, we stress, are given meanings by human actors, both as senders and receivers. What we haven't done, I think (or at least we haven't done it well), is apply this sociological insight about the world at large to our own courses and classrooms. It is time for us to acknowledge that a great deal of the emphasis that we give to common complaints about students' lack of writing skills is misplaced; in fact, it is largely backwards. Instead of stating that students need to "learn to write," we need to be providing more opportunities for them to "write to learn."

No one can deny, of course, the role of proper grammar and punctuation in readability, and the contribution to precision of meaning of standard paragraph structure and the use of complete sentences and correct spelling. To have these as our primary focus, however, misses the point. What do we really want students to learn in their sociology courses? I think most of us would agree that we want students to emerge from these courses with a mastery of basic sociological concepts and theories and an ability to apply them appropriately to their lives and society. Since the 1960s many, if not most, sociologists have wholeheartedly subscribed to C. Wright Mills' dictum that sociology should help us to "understand personal troubles as public issues." While it is easy enough for us to articulate the social forces and structures behind public issues, it is much harder, in my experience, to assist students in making the connections to their own lives, or "personal troubles." Yet, the establishment of those links is absolutely necessary if we are to move students, in William Perry's familiar scheme, from simplistic dualism to committed relativism (see Resources section at the end).

This is where writing can play a valuable role. Done properly, writing in sociology courses can not only help students to work through their understanding of the basic concepts, but it can provide the space for them to think through the application of these concepts to their own lives. Moreover, writing assignments can be tailored to affirm both the legitimacy and the necessity of students developing intelligent, informed opinions of their own. In short, writing can help students to "find their voices."

The difficulty of this task, though, should not be underestimated. In some of my first forays into student writing other than essay exams and term papers, I quickly discovered that unexpectedly large numbers of students were unable (unwilling?) to discuss personal experiences and express personal values. For instance, in one assignment students were asked to state their view of human nature and their basic values. I carefully stressed that I would not grade them on their views, but on only the extensiveness and clarity with which they stated them. Yet many students — even after two or three rewrites — insisted on writing detached, seemingly "objective" "social problem analysis" papers. They apparently felt that their real opinion was unimportant for purposes of their education. (Or that they dare not reveal their true opinion under pain of a bad grade.) More telling perhaps was my experience with senior-level students. Asked to develop personal criteria by which to evaluate theories and policies, they responded that this was too difficult because no one had ever really asked them their own opinion before and they had no skill in expressing it.

Casting about for a way to get students to connect their own stories to the content of sociological analysis, I was referred to *The Call of Stories* by Robert Coles. Author of the acclaimed *Women of Crisis* and *Children of Crisis* book series, Coles is an acknowledged expert at listening to people's voices as they tell their own stories. In *The Call of Stories*, Coles describes his experience teaching in graduate medical, law, and business schools, where his "textbooks" consisted entirely of short stories and novels. Through their writing and discussion, students were able to develop insights, make connections and render moral judgments that often surprised Coles in their depth and richness. His book stands as both a compelling argument as well as a resource for using literature in social science courses as a way of helping students to "find their voices."

One advantage of using fiction in sociology courses is that it is more immediately accessible to students. Because the stories have been "engineered" by the authors to be emotionally compelling, they draw students in and involve them in ways that are unavailable to even the best discursive writing. Indeed, this affective component represents one of the most neglected areas of college teaching, in my opinion. And precisely because the stories are fiction, students often seem far more willing to seriously consider the sociological issues raised than they would be from documentary nonfiction.

Another advantage of using fiction in sociology courses is that it provides instructors with an opportunity to ensure the representation in their classrooms of a variety of voices from divergent viewpoints. While this process and its results are pedagogically desirable under any circumstances, they become absolutely necessary in the diverse, multicultural environment of contemporary colleges and universities. Exposing students to multiple voices not only expands their sociological understanding, but it legitimates the diversity of life experiences and viewpoints we now encounter within the classroom. It empowers less-traditional students by acknowledging that their stories are also worth listening to.

How does a sympathetic teacher identify and locate quality fiction that represents diverse viewpoints? Fortunately, a variety of multicultural anthologies are now available. Such readers feature the works of authors typically excluded from the mainstream — e.g., women, racial and ethnic minorities, and working-class authors. One resource I use in my classes is *The Heath Anthology of American Literature*. This two-volume work (each about 2500 pages, available separately) represents a progressive response to the "canon wars" that have been fought in literature circles over the past several decades. In addition to the acknowledged "classics" (largely written by white males), The *Heath Anthology* attempts to integrate the voices and stories of the excluded — African-American, Hispanic, Native American, and female and working-class writers of all ethnic persuasions — into an exploration of the American experience. The result is a rich treasury of sociological themes. A number of other current literary collections accomplish this same task as well. Check with literature faculty on your campus.

Even while acknowledging the value of doing so, many sociology instructors are going to be uncomfortable with the thought of having students write about literary works. "I am not a literary critic," you say. This may be true, but you don't have to be. After all, you are using the literature to illustrate and provoke thinking about sociological themes, and this is something you already know. Discussions of plot, theme, and characterization are secondary, if not mostly irrelevant to this purpose. (See the Appendix for two examples of this approach.) On the other hand, we might actually benefit, in our teaching and our own writing, by a better understanding of the insights of literature instructors. The more I talk with colleagues in literature, the more I am convinced that much of what they teach is actually sociology. Couldn't both we and they benefit from a fruitful exchange of ideas and insights? Resources to aid in this process include the Teacher's Manual that accompanies *The Heath Anthology*.

Another objection that can be raised is the potentially enormous time commitment involved in assigning and evaluating a significant amount of writing in our courses. In times of rising course sizes and increasing class loads, this is no idle protest. Yet, the evaluation of writing does not have to be excessively burdensome for either the students or the instructor. First of all, not all student writing has to be evaluated for a grade — student journals, for example, where the emphasis is on the student processing the information and providing a thoughtful response and the instructor providing substantive feedback on that response. Where grading is deemed to be necessary and appropriate, it can be significantly streamlined by stating the specific assignment clearly, and providing relatively simple and explicit criteria for evaluation. (See examples of writing assignments and the sample syllabus in the Appendix.)

I don't for a minute wish to suggest that this is the only, or even the best way to address writing in the sociology curriculum. But providing opportunities for students to find and express their voices, and to acknowledge the legitimacy of diverse "stories" is a way of dealing with two of the most pressing pedagogical issues we face today: improving the writing/thinking skills of our students, and recognizing and dealing with the increasing diversity of our students.

USING THIS INSTRUCTOR'S MANUAL

The rest of this Instructor's Manual is designed to assist you in actually delivering the course to students. The information should be used, as noted earlier, in conjunction with the Study Guide built into the textbook. Some of this Manual recapitulates the Study Guide, but in a different form and to a different end. For instance, each chapter of the Instructor's Manual begins with a complete outline of the text chapter, including all bold-faced subheads. This is necessary because the outline at the beginning of each text chapter is only partial — it includes only two levels. Also included are the titles for all boxed items.

Next the Instructor's Manual catalogs the learning objectives for a chapter, followed by a listing of all the Key Concepts divided by major subhead and, if applicable, a list of Key Thinkers/Researchers from the Study Guide. However, unlike the Study Guide where the order of the concepts and people is scrambled for pedagogical purposes, here the concepts and thinkers are listed in the same order in which they appear in the text. The definitions or descriptions, however, match those that appear in the Study Guide matching exercise. This makes it easy for an instructor to be knowledgeable about what the students are studying.

Next comes material unique to the Instructor's Manual. First there are Lecture Suggestions — a series of ideas for conveying the text material to students in the most interesting and effective fashion. Then there are Suggested Activities — things that you may want to do in class and/or assign students to do out of class to practice applying basic sociological concepts to their own lives. Finally there is the Resources section. First are listed books and other sources to help organize your own thinking on important concepts. Then there is an annotated bibliography of suggested readings for students, designed as either a resource for the instructor or a handout for the curious student. The books have been selected for their accessibility to introductory-level students; the annotations are designed both to give students a flavor of what the book is about and to draw them in to reading one or more of them. Given the limitations of space, I was not able to include all of my favorites. I'm sure I didn't include all of yours, either. Nonetheless, if you share this listing with students, it will hopefully pique their curiosity, and they will ask you — or you can make a point of telling them — about other books as well.

A few final words of advice. Relax and enjoy yourself. Remember, you are teaching students about what is, for most of them, the most fascinating subject possible: themselves and their society. If you are enthusiastic about the usefulness of sociological skills and understandings, it will likely become contagious. Don't be afraid to let your own personality and interests shine through. The materials in this Instructor's Manual are meant only as a starting point. Shape them to fit your own style and approach. Take some risks and try new things. Things may not work as you planned, but in teaching, as in research, we learn as much or more from our failures as from our successes. Have fun and do good work!

RESOURCES FOR INSTRUCTORS

American Sociological Association Teaching Resources Center, 1722 N Street NW, Washington, D.C. 20036. Voice: (202) 833-3410 Fax: (202) 785-0146 E-mail: asa_academic_professional_affairs@mcimail.com
  Probably the single most valuable source of information on teaching sociology. Write, call, or fax for a free catalog. They offer syllabi sets and resource sets for just about every sociology course, as well as resources on classroom discussion techniques, suggested videos and films, using humor in teaching sociology, etc.

Books on Teaching and Pedagogy

Benjamin S. Bloom, et al., *Taxonomy of Educational Objectives: Cognitive Domain.* New York: David Mckay Co., 1956.
  A timeless classic, it describes a hierarchy of intellectual processes and the objectives that go with them. Useful for thinking about how to design a course to move students beyond the levels of knowledge and understanding, to application, analysis, and evaluation.

Kenneth Eble, *The Craft of Teaching: A Guide to Mastering the Professor's Art, 2nd ed.* San Francisco: Jossey-Bass, 1988.
  A manifesto on teaching as an art that can be learned; good chapters on learning to teach.

Barbara S. Fuhrmann and Anthony F. Grasha, *A Practical Handbook for College Teachers.* Boston: Little, Brown, 1983.
  A useful attempt to gather a great deal of practical information on college teaching in one place.

Margaret Morganroth Gullette, ed., The Art and Craft of Teaching. Cambridge, Mass.: Harvard University Press, 1984.
  A collection of insightful and helpful essays originally published by the Harvard-Danforth Center for Teaching and Learning.

Bruce A. Kimball, ed., *Teaching Undergraduates: Essays from the Lilly Endowment Workshop on the Liberal Arts.* Buffalo, NY: Prometheus Books, 1988.
> A collection of essays from the staff of the Lilly Workshop. The authors have years of experience teaching and teaching teachers to teach.

Robert F. Mager, *Preparing Instructional Objectives, rev. 2nd ed.* Belmont, CA: David S. Lake, 1984.
> Entertaining and witty, this practical manual is brief and to the point. If you can't write behavioral objectives after reading this book, you haven't been paying attention.

Wilbert J. McKeachie, *Teaching Tips: A Guidebook for the Beginning College Teacher, 8th ed.* Lexington, MA: D.C. Heath, 1986.
> One of the best discussions of all the role behaviors expected of college teachers.

William Perry, *Intellectual and Ethical Development in the College Years: A Scheme.* New York: Holt, 1970.
> A classic, it lays out a scheme for understanding student intellectual growth, from simplistic dualism to complex relativism. Important for thinking about goals and objectives, especially in areas like sociology that deal with social problems.

Periodicals on Teaching and Pedagogy

The Teaching Professor. Published ten times per year by Magna Publications, Inc., 2718 Dryden Drive, Madison, WI 53704-3086. $34 for one year.
> Each newsletter consists of a series of short, practical articles including research summaries, description of teaching techniques, short discussions of pedagogical issues, and comments. Very useful.

Teaching Sociology. Published quarterly by the American Sociological Association, 1722 N Street, N.W., Washington, D.C. 20036. ASA Member rate: $20 for one year; nonmembers $27 for one year.
> Includes research articles, teaching tips, discussions, and book, software, and film reviews.

Teaching Contrasting Perspectives

Gary Alan Fine, *Talking Sociology, 3rd ed.* Boston: Allyn and Bacon, 1993.
> Compares and contrasts libertarian, conservative, and social democratic perspectives on eleven "hot" contemporary social issues, then presents current sociological research on the issue. Conversationally written and accessible to introductory students.

Resources for Using Writing in Sociology Courses

Robert Coles, *The Call of Stories: Teaching and the Moral Imagination.* Boston: Houghton Mifflin, 1989.
> The author's personal narrative of his experience using literature to teach social science. Provides a powerful argument for using literature in sociology as well as some good examples of how to do it. Also suggests that one of our primary roles as teachers is to learn to listen to students' stories.

Paul Lauter (Gen. Ed.). *The Heath Anthology of American Literature.* 2 volumes. Lexington, MA.: D.C. Heath, 1990.
A comprehensive and diverse collection of short stories, poems, speeches, and essays on the American experience. Each author is placed in social and historical context. A terrific source of material for sociology courses.

RESOURCES FOR STUDENTS

Nicholas Abercrombie, Stephen Hill, and Bryan S. Turner, *The Penguin Dictionary of Sociology, 2nd ed.* New York: Penguin, 1988.
A handy paperback that is surprisingly comprehensive in its coverage of concepts, theories, theorists, and methodologies.

Inge Bell, *This Book is Not Required, rev. ed.* Fort Bragg, CA: The Small Press, 1990. (707) 937-3044
A college survival manual for students. Sensitively written by someone who obviously cares a great deal about students and their education, this book tells students the "inside scoop" on what college is all about. It's the sort of stuff sophisticated college students learn and share; we as professors tend forget, however, that many of our students don't know it. Yet they need this information. This book can provide it.

Lee Cuba, *A Short Guide to Writing About Social Science, 2nd ed.* New York: HarperCollins, 1993.
Another good resource guide for students. This one is focused more on the process of researching, organizing, and writing the paper.

The Sociology Writing Group, *A Guide to Writing Sociology Papers.* New York: St. Martin's, 1986.
For students, an excellent paperback guide to getting organized and writing library research, textual analysis, ethnographic, and quantitative research papers.

APPENDIX

SAMPLE SYLLABUS FOR INTRODUCTORY SOCIOLOGY

Instructor: Patrick J. Ashton, Ph.D.
Office: CM 235   Phone: 219 481-6669
Hours: TTh 12:00 – 1:30 pm, 7 - 7:30 pm
            or by appointment

Fall 1995
Indiana University-Purdue University Fort Wayne

COURSE DESCRIPTION AND OBJECTIVES

Sociology is the scientific study of human society and social interaction. All of us, of course, already have considerable experience living in society and interacting with other people. Sociology, however, is an unfamiliar way of looking at the familiar. It should help us understand our experience in a more critical way, and therefore to use that experience more effectively. As an introduction to the discipline of sociology, this course is organized as a **skills** as well as a **survey** class. That is, in addition to acquainting you with the basic concepts used by sociologists to explain the social world and social interaction, the course will give you elementary skills with which to "decode" society and social life — i.e., the skills to **understand** the social world in order to **change** it in ways you find appropriate. The basic skills you will learn in this course include the ability to:

•describe, analyze, and contrast the basic value positions, or perspectives, which generate and shape our goals;

•deconstruct and analyze the basic processes of social life, which includes developing a critical understanding of the social research methods by which we discover these processes; and

•comprehend the pattern and direction of social change.

More specifically, when you have completed this course you should be able to:

1. Identify and explain the four major perspectives on contemporary social issues in the United States: Organic Conservative, Individualist Conservative, Reform Liberal, and Socialist/Radical. To explain means to be able to spell out the basic assumptions, major policies, and orientation to change of each perspective.

2. Critically evaluate social science research data.

3. Explain and appropriately apply basic sociological concepts.

4. Identify and explain basic human needs and the social situations that inhibit as well as those that contribute to the satisfaction of these basic needs.

5. Describe and explain the basic dimensions of social inequality in contemporary society and the current trajectories of change.

6. Specify your own perspective on the social world and explain how and why you came to possess this outlook.

COURSE FORMAT AND POLICIES

Class Meetings. I will make every reasonable effort to help you be successful in this course. If you want to learn about sociology, I want to help you do it (and to certify at the end that you have in fact done so). Class meetings will be organized on a lecture/discussion basis, with **questions, comments, and discussion encouraged during all class meetings.** If there is something you don't understand, ask about it right then — don't wait till later. A short period of time will be reserved at the beginning of each class period to answer questions and clarify issues from previous class sessions that, upon review, were unclear or confusing to you. Have your questions and comments ready. Class meetings will also include activities (for example, videos, small discussion groups, games) designed to help you learn course material. Ultimately, how much you learn and remember from this course is closely related to how much you can relate it to your own life. I urge you to make these connections as much as possible, and to share your insights with others.

An outline of each class period's activity will be written on the board prior to that class. In addition, a list of basic concepts from both the lectures and the readings will be handed out at the beginning of each section of the course. Class attendance is not mandatory, but it is highly recommended, as the lectures will regularly provide information not available in the readings. If you miss a lecture, you should try to get the notes from a classmate. I have no objection if you wish to tape record lectures.

Active Learning. The key to being a successful student is *active learning,* and your textbook is designed to stimulate and encourage this approach. Pay particular attention to the essay, "A Word to the Student: How to Get the Most out of Sociology," that begins on page xi in the front of the book. It contains valuable tips on how to be a successful student — e.g., how to read and study effectively, how to function effectively in class, how to successfully take tests. This information is based on the research of developmental learning specialists and is proven effective. If you haven't learned these tips already, master them now. They are keys to your success as a student!

Study Groups. I encourage you to form study groups with other students enrolled in this class. Many successful students report that the discussions that take place in these groups are valuable in helping them to identify and reinforce important course material. Students also say that group participation helps them to better understand the material through comparing the differing cognitive approaches of group members and the different ways the course material relates to each individual's life. The groups can also be valuable sources of social and emotional support.

Using the Textbook. As you can see from the Table of Contents, your textbook is divided into five main parts. Each part begins with a short essay that tells what will be addressed in that section of the book, how each chapter is interrelated, and how the current section builds on the previous section(s) and how it prepares you for information to come in other sections. Prior to reading a chapter in the book you are advised to read the relevant Part Opener to put that chapter in context.

The Study Guide at the back of your textbook (identified with colored-edge pages) is designed in workbook fashion to give you practice in actively learning and applying important concepts. Every student is encouraged to do the Study Guide exercises as a means of really comprehending and assimilating the text material. You can test your knowledge of main points further by taking each chapter's Practice Test, which will be found with the other Practice Tests following the Study Guide.

Writing. Writing will play an important role in this course, as it is my view that the manipulation of ideas required in the process of writing is a crucial element of critical thinking and analysis. Writing out the Study Guide exercises is one way to develop and practice this skill. You are also encouraged to rewrite your lecture notes, preferably as soon as possible after class. In addition, I will give you a variety of short writing assignments, both in-class and take-home. Some of these assignments will be evaluated for a grade, as noted later.

Accommodating Disabilities. If you have or acquire any sort of disability that may require accommodation, I urge you to discuss it with me (preferably after class or during office hours). I want to do everything that I can to help everyone who wants to succeed in this course. If you want to find out what special services and accommodations are available on campus, you are encouraged to contact the campus Services for Students with Disabilities office.

COURSE MATERIAL

The following books are **required** and are available for purchase in the campus bookstore. Several copies are also on reserve at the Circulation Desk in the campus Library.

Henry L. Tischler, *Introduction to Sociology, Fifth Edition*. The Harcourt Press, 1996.
Gary Alan Fine, *Talking Sociology, Third Edition*. Allyn and Bacon, 1993.

Please make every attempt to do the assigned reading *before* coming to class. There are a number of benefits to doing so: (1) you will be prepared to ask questions; and (2) you will already be somewhat familiar with the material, so that information covered in class should seem less confusing to you, and the instructor will not seem to be speaking as fast.

METHOD OF EVALUATION

Your performance in this course will be evaluated on the basis of 4 in-class exams and 6 writing assignments, described as follows:

EXAMS: Each exam will consist of 60 multiple-choice questions worth one point each. The exams will be given in class on the dates noted below. They will **not** be cumulative; that is, each exam will cover only the material presented in the segment of the course immediately preceding it, as noted below. Approximately half of the questions on each exam will be taken from in-class material (including videos, discussions, etc.) and half from the readings. **All questions will be drawn from the material listed on the Basic Concepts handout.** An in-class preparation for the exam will take place during the class period immediately prior to each exam.

If you miss an exam for any reason, please contact me *as soon as possible,* **so that other arrangements can be made.**

Exam #	Given in Class on	Covering Material From
1	Sept 22	Weeks 1 – 4
2	Oct 20	Weeks 5 – 8
3	Nov 17	Weeks 9 – 12
4	Dec 17	Weeks 13 –16

WRITING ASSIGNMENTS: During the course of the term you will be given six different take-home writing assignments. In each assignment you will be asked to analyze course material and/or relate it to your own life. Your completed papers should be **no longer than 2-3 pages, typed or computer-printed.** Students have access to a number of computer labs on campus, and some consulting assistance is available. Handwritten papers will not be accepted.

Your papers should adhere to all appropriate rules of organization, spelling, and grammar — i.e., they should be formatted in complete sentences and paragraphs, have an introduction, body, and conclusion, etc. The writing assignments will be evaluated, in general, on two criteria: (1) clarity of exposition [do you make a point and make it clearly?], and (2) extent to which you use course material relevant to the assigned topic. You are encouraged to discuss the writing assignment topics among yourselves, but each student must write and submit their own unique paper.

GRADING

Exams. Each of the exams will be graded as percent correct out of 60 questions and will count as 10% of your grade. The four exams combined will count as 40% of your final grade.

Writing Assignments. The writing assignments will be graded on the following scale:

88-100	Outstanding use and application of course materials; comprehensive coverage
78-87	Above-average use and application of course material, but some details are lacking
68-77	Appropriate use & application of course materials, but significant gaps/omissions exist
58-67	Some effort made to use course materials, but major flaws are present
≤ 57	Missed the point altogether or misunderstood the assignment completely

I reserve the right to deduct points for flagrantly improper grammar, spelling, and/or punctuation. Each writing assignment will count as 12% of your grade. The 5 writing assignments together will count as 60% of your final grade.

Grading Summary: 4 exams @ 10% each =   40% of final grade
                        5 papers @ 12% each =   <u>60%</u> of final grade
                                                100%

Final grades for the course will be assigned according to the following scale:

A	=	88% - 100%
B	=	78% - 87%
C	=	68% - 77%
D	=	58% - 67%
F	=	57% & below

There will be no curve, and no extra-credit work.

TOPIC OUTLINE AND READING ASSIGNMENTS

<u>Week</u>	<u>Date</u>	<u>Reading Assignment and Lecture Topic</u>
1	Aug 25	Philosophy, Overview & Organization of the Course

   Reading: Tischler, Chapter 1, pp. 1-10

| | Aug 27 | What Is Sociology? |

<u>Week</u>	<u>Date</u>	<u>Reading Assignment and Lecture Topic</u>
2		**Reading:** Tischler, Chapter 1, pp. 10-23; Chapter 19, pp. 411-419
	Sept 1	The Development of Sociology
	Sept 3	Sociological Theorists and Theoretical Perspectives
3		**Reading:** Fine, "Introduction," pp. 1-17; Chapter Four, pp. 68-82
	Sept 8	Contemporary Ideological Perspectives
	Sept 10	Applying the Perspectives
4		**Reading:** Tischler, Chapter 2, pp. 25-41
	Sept 15	Introduction to Social Research Methods
	Sept 17	Research Methodology
5	**Sept 22**	**EXAM #1**
		Reading: Tischler, Chapter 4, pp. 69-74
		Fine, Chapter Eight, pp. 136-150
	Sept 24	The Nature of Human Nature
6		**Reading:** Tischler, Chapter 3, pp. 42-66; Chapter 5, pp. 93-117
	Sept 29	Culture and Human Nature/Social Organization
	Oct 1	Culture and Social Groups
7		**Reading:** Tischler, Chapter 6, pp. 119-147
		Fine, Chapter Three, pp. 51-65
	Oct 6	Institutions and Social Control
	Oct 8	**NO CLASS — Fall Break**
8		**Reading:** Tischler, Chapter 4, pp. 74-91
		Fine, Chapter One, pp. 19-32
	Oct 13	Fundamentals of Socialization
	Oct 15	Socialization and the Self
9	**Oct 20**	**EXAM #2**
		Reading: Fine, Chapter Two, pp. 35-48; Chapter Ten, pp. 171-184
	Oct 22	Institutionalization and Socialization: Conditions for Self-Actualization

Week	Date	Reading Assignment and Lecture Topic

October 25 — Last day to officially withdraw from course

10

                                   Reading: Tischler, Chapter 13, pp. 291-307
                                                      Fine, Chapter Nine, pp. 154-168

      Oct 27   Institutionalization and Socialization: Education
      Oct 29   Institutionalization and Socialization: Sex and Gender

11

                                     Reading: Fine, Chapter Six, pp. 103-116
                                                        Tischler, Chapter 10, pp. 215-231; Chapter 8, pp. 169-185

      Nov 3   Language, Institutions, and Gender
      Nov 5   Economic Inequality in the U.S.

12

                                     Reading: Tischler, Chapter 14, pp. 309-329; Chapter 7, pp. 151-167

      Nov 10   Comparative Inequality and Social Mobility
      Nov 12   Perspectives on Inequality

13   Nov 17   **EXAM #3**

                                   Reading: Tischler, Chapter 9, pp. 187-212

      Nov 19   The Ethnic Hierarchy

14

                                     Reading: Fine, Chapter Seven, pp. 118-133

      Nov 24   Dimensions of Racial and Ethnic Inequality
      Nov 26   **NO CLASS -- THANKSGIVING!!!**

15

                                     Reading: Tischler, Chapter 15, pp. 333-351; Chapter 19, pp. 419-421

      Dec 1   Underdevelopment in the Third World
      Dec 3   Perspectives on Underdevelopment

16

                                     Reading: Tischler, Chapter 18, pp. 393-409; Chapter 19, pp. 421-422
                                                        Fine, Chapter Twelve, pp. 203-216

      Dec 8   International Inequality and Social Change
      Dec 10   Processes and Trajectories of Social Change

EXAM #4   Sec 3677 Thursday, December 17, 1:00 pm
                                    Sec 3681 Thursday, December 17, 8:30 pm   Course Evaluations

SOC S161 Principles of Sociology   Fall 1995
Patrick J. Ashton

BASIC CONCEPTS FOR EXAM #2

ISSUES FROM THE LECTURES

Nature of Human Nature: 2 defining characteristics
    evidence: prehistoric; infants/children; adults

Culture: society's symbolic system
    symbol: an arbitrary, shared representation
    language: symbolic communication
    relationship of culture to biology
    ethnocentrism: judging other cultures by the standards of one's own culture
    cultural relativism: Judging each culture by its own standards
        Basic Human Needs: universal, unique, and objective
            2 reasons for using the concept
                1) Provides an objective standard of comparison among societies and subcultures
                2) Provides a basis for analyzing conflict and change
            Maslow's Hierarchy of Needs

material culture: artifacts
nonmaterial culture
    norms: shared rules of conduct
        folkways: conventions of everyday life
        mores: customs with moral overtones
        taboos: absolute moral prohibitions
    values: criteria for judging what is appropriate, moral or desirable
    knowledge: ideas for which we have some empirical evidence
    beliefs: ideas for which we do not have empirical evidence

Social structure: the patterned framework of social life
    status: a socially-defined position within the social structure
        status set: all the statuses occupied by an individual at a given time
        master status: the dominant status occupied by an individual at a given time
        ascribed status vs. achieved status
    role: behavioral expectations associated with a position (status)
        role set: all of the roles attached to a single status

Groups: sets of people who interact on the basis of shared expectations
    primary vs. secondary groups

Institution: a standardized solution to a collective problem
    habit: a standardized solution to an individual problem
    basic institutions
    Institutions imply history and control
    Institutions channel behavior and awareness

External (Direct) vs. Internal (Indirect) Social Control
    external social control: based on outward behavioral compliance

19

ISSUES FROM THE LECTURES (cont.)

internal social control: based upon individual monitoring of one's own behavior

deviance: a violation of social expectations that is recognized and defined as such
       functions (4)
       dysfunctions (3)

Primary Socialization: the process by which a biological infant becomes a conscious, social being
      Why is it primary?
         •first
         •foundation
         •primary groups
      Functions:
         •social reproduction
         •internalization of social control
         •creation of the self
      key factor: socio-emotional bonds (social attachments)
      socialization and Symbolic Interaction: the 2 roles of language
         — function of egocentric speech in development

      Compare and integrate (see handout):
         Mead's stages of progressive role-taking ability (5)
         Piaget's stages of cognitive development (4)
         Erikson's stages of childhood development (5)
      Functions of the Primary Care-Givers (3) — see handout
      Styles of Primary Socialization (3) — see handout

The Looking-Glass Self — 3 components (see reading also)
Self, Core Self-Image, Self-Esteem, Situated Social Identities — definitions and relationship of
      components
      impression management or "facework"
         studied nonobservance
         civil inattention
         aligning actions

ISSUES FROM THE READINGS

Tischler, Chapter 4, pp. 69-74
      instincts — definition
      conditioning — definition
      effects of extreme childhood deprivation
         Examples: Victor; Genie; Harlow's research; infants in institutions
      social attachments — definition
      affiliation — definition, importance

Fine, Chapter Eight, pp. 136-150
      3 perspectives on who should be allowed to adopt children

ISSUES FROM THE READINGS (cont)

<u>Tischler, Chapter 3, pp. 42-66</u>
    culture shock — e.g., Chagnon and the Yanomamö
    ethnocentrism
    cultural relativism
    components of culture:
        material culture
        nonmaterial culture
            normative culture (norms)
             mores vs. folkways
            ideal vs. real norms
            cognitive culture
            [knowledge and beliefs]
            values
        relationship between material and nonmaterial culture
    mechanisms of cultural change: innovation and diffusion
    adaptation
    cultural lag
    qualities of culture (p. 54)
    signs vs. symbols
    selectivity [categorization]
    Do animals have culture?
    subculture
    cultural universals (4)
    culture and individual choice [repression]

<u>Tischler, Chapter 5, pp. 93-117</u>
    social interaction — definition
    influence of context and norms on social interaction
    types of social interaction (5)
    statuses
        master status
        achieved vs. ascribed status
    roles
        role sets
        role strain/conflict
        role playing — implications
        role enactment
    social group vs. social aggregate
    primary vs. secondary groups
    reference group
    small groups — e.g., dyad, triad
    large groups — associations
    formal vs. informal organizational structure
    bureaucracy — definition

<u>Fine, Chapter Three, pp. 51-65</u>
    ideological social control — definition
    3 perspectives on the legalization of drugs

ISSUES FROM THE READINGS (cont)

Tischler, Chapter 6, pp. 119-147
> moral code
> normal vs. deviant behavior
> functions of deviance
> dysfunctions of deviance
> internal vs. external means of control
>> sanctions — definition; types(4) — see Figure 6-1; examples of each

Tischler, Chapter 4, pp. 74-91
> personality — definition
> social identity — definition
> self — definition
> Piaget: stages of cognitive development (4)
> looking-glass theory — 3 stages
> Mead: stages of self-development
> significant others — definition
> Erikson's 5 stages of childhood development
> most important agents of childhood socialization (4)
> primary socialization vs. adult socialization
> resocialization — definition
>> total institutions — definition, factors of effectiveness
> impact of day care on infants and young children

Fine, Chapter One, pp. 19-32
> cultural absolutism vs. cultural relativity
> linguistic relativity (or Sapir-Whorf) hypothesis — basic thesis
> 3 perspectives on bilingual education

S161 Principles of Sociology   Fall 1995
Patrick J. Ashton

SAMPLE WRITING ASSIGNMENT #1

Length: 2-3 pages
Due: Tuesday, September 8

Purpose: This assignment is designed to allow you to develop skill in applying the sociological imagination.

Assignment: Read the short story "Lullaby" by Leslie Silko [in *The Heath Anthology*] and discuss some of the social forces and/or conditions that affected the lives of Ayah and Chato by answering *each* of the following questions:

•What kinds of power are exercised in this story? Who has the power? What is the basis of that power? On whom is it exercised?

•Ethnocentrism is the (inappropriate) use of the standards of our own culture to judge the beliefs and practices of another culture. How is ethnocentrism manifest in this story?

•What role does language play in the experiences of Ayah and Chato in this story?

•Can you relate the experience of the characters in this story to any aspect of your own life? Why or why not?

Evaluation: Papers will be evaluated on how thoroughly and thoughtfully each question is answered and the extent to which you employ the sociological imagination as it is described in class and in the readings.

Grading: Papers will be graded according to the scale in the course outline.

23

S161 Principles of Sociology   Fall 1995
Patrick J. Ashton

SAMPLE WRITING ASSIGNMENT #2

Length: 2–3 pages
Due: Thursday, October 3

Purpose: To help you gain further skill in understanding and applying basic sociological concepts.

Assignment: Choose three concepts or sets of concepts from the list below. Using standard essay form, illustrate each of the concepts by relating it to a situation, incident or experience from your own life. In your discussion you should be sure to (1) be brief, but give enough details about the experience to make it understandable to the reader, and (2) explain why the experience is an example of the concept you have chosen (that is, relate the definition of the concept to the description of the experience).

> ideal vs. real norms
> subculture
> signals vs. signs vs. symbols
> ascribed vs. achieved status
> role conflict
> primary vs. secondary groups
> reference group
> formal vs. informal organizational structure
> internal vs. external means of control

Evaluation: Papers will be evaluated on the extent to which the basic sociological concepts are appropriately and thoughtfully applied.

Grading: Papers will be graded according to the scale in the course outline.

CHAPTER ONE: The Sociological Perspective

CHAPTER OUTLINE

Sociology as a Point of View
    The Sociological Imagination
    Taking the Sociological Perspective: If You Are Thinking About Sociology as a Career, Read This
    Is Sociology Common Sense?
    Sociology and Science
    Sociology as a Social Science
        Cultural Anthropology
        Psychology
        Economics
        History
        Political Science
        Social Work

The Development of Sociology
    Auguste Comte (1798 - 1857)
    Harriet Martineau (1802 - 1876)
    Herbert Spencer (1820 – 1903)
    Karl Marx (1818 – 1883)
    Émile Durkheim (1858 – 1917)
    Max Weber (1864 – 1920)

The Development of Sociology in the United States
    Sociology at Work: Women and the Development of Sociology, 1800 to 1945

Theoretical Perspectives
    Functionalism
    Conflict Theory
    The Interactionist Perspective
        Symbolic Interactionism
        Ethnomethodology
        Dramaturgy
    Contemporary Sociology
    Theory and Practice
    Controversies in Sociology: Is There a Difference Between Sociology and Journalism?

LEARNING OBJECTIVES

1. Understand and explain the sociological point of view.

2. Explain how the sociological point of view differs from that of journalists and talk show hosts.

3. Explain why sociology is a social science.

4. Compare and contrast sociology with the other major social sciences.

5. Trace the early development of sociology from its origins in nineteenth-century Europe.

6. Summarize the major contributions of sociology's pioneers: Comte, Martineau, Spencer, Marx, Durkheim, and Weber.

7. Describe the early development of sociology in the United States.

8. Describe and contrast functionalism, conflict theory, and the interactionist perspective.

9. Explain the major contemporary interactionist perspectives: symbolic interactionism, ethnomethodology, and dramaturgy.

10. Explain the connection between theory and practice.

KEY CONCEPTS

Sociology as a Point of View

sociology: the scientific study of human society and social interactions.

the sociological imagination: the process of looking at all types of human behavior patterns and discerning unseen connections among them.

science: a body of systematically arranged knowledge that shows the operation of general laws.

the scientific method: the building of knowledge through systematic observation, experimentation, generalization, and verification.

empiricism: the view that generalizations are valid only if they rely on evidence that can be observed directly or verified through our senses.

the social sciences: those disciplines that apply scientific methods to the study of human behavior.

Social Darwinism: the notion that people who cannot successfully compete in modern society are poorly adapted to their environment and therefore inferior.

The Development of Sociology in the United States

social functions: processes that contribute to the ongoing operation or maintenance of society.

manifest functions: intended and recognized consequences of social processes.

latent functions: unintended or not readily recognized consequences of social processes.

Theoretical Perspectives

paradigm: a model or framework for organizing the questions that generate and guide research.

functionalism: a view of society as a system of highly interrelated parts that operate together rather harmoniously.

conflict theory: a view of society that sees it constantly changing in response to social inequality and the resulting conflict.

interactionist perspective: a view that focuses on how individuals make sense of the social world.

symbolic interactionism: a view that is concerned with the meanings that people place on their own and one another's behavior.

ethnomethodology: the study of the rules that individuals use to initiate, respond to, and modify behavior in social settings.

dramaturgy: the study of the way that individuals use roles to create impressions in social settings.

middle-range theories: theories that are concerned with explaining specific issues or aspects of society rather than how all of the society operates.

KEY THINKERS/RESEARCHERS

C. Wright Mills: developed the concept of the sociological imagination.

Auguste Comte: coined the term sociology and tried to show how the new discipline would improve society.

Harriet Martineau: analyzed the customs and lifestyles of the nineteenth-century United States in a comprehensive, comparative, and objective way.

Herbert Spencer: developed many of the standard terms and concepts of sociology and wrote them down in the first sociology textbook; advocate of Social Darwinism.

Karl Marx: pioneered the conflict theory approach to sociology; tried to understand the social forces that produced inequality and class conflict and sought to improve the human condition.

Émile Durkheim: the first professor of sociology; produced the first true sociological study, in which the individual act of suicide was explained as a result of social forces.

Max Weber: showed that religion as a belief system could contribute to the creation of new economic conditions and institutions; pioneered the study of bureaucracy.

the Chicago School: early U.S. sociologists who developed empirical methods for studying urban neighborhoods and ethnic areas.

W.E.B. DuBois: extensively investigated the history and sociology of African Americans.

Talcott Parsons: an early U.S. sociologist who elaborated functionalist theory and advocated a value-free approach to sociology.

Robert K. Merton: an advocate of functionalism who developed the distinction between manifest and latent functions.

George Herbert Mead: first developed the symbolic interactionist perspective.

Harold Garfinkel: proposed the ethnomethodological approach to studying social behavior.

Erving Goffman: developed dramaturgy as a way of studying social interaction.

Lewis Coser: incorporated aspects of functionalism and conflict theory in viewing conflict as both functional and dysfunctional.

LECTURE SUGGESTIONS

1. **Definition of Sociology.** In the Resources section at the end of this chapter is a suggested handout or overhead regarding the definition of sociology. You can see that it resolves into four components: science, humans, patterns, and groups. Many would argue that it is *science* that sets sociology apart from social philosophy. *Human* equals social and symbolic because these seem to be the two basic characteristics of human nature — i.e., what it means to be human. Society implies *patterns* because a society is relatively large and persists over time. Therefore it must have patterns — of organization, thought, and behavior. And if it has patterns we can study it systematically. Also, if we learn enough about the origin and persistence of patterns, we have the possibility of changing them. Social interaction implies *groups* because interaction (*inter* is Latin for *between*) can only take place between two or more people; the smallest unit of analysis in sociology is the group (and therefore at least a dyad). These leads to the importance of group influence as sociology's basic insight. Students socialized in American society are likely to resist this concept. Tell them that, this early in the course, it's okay — you've got the rest of the term to try to convince them of the important role of groups in people's lives. And then make sure you work to actually convince them! Emphasizing the four components of the definition of sociology is a handy way to preface some basic issues about sociology and its perspective, and throughout the term you can refer back to these four components as a touchstone.

2. **The Sociological Imagination.** Most introductory students are unused to seeing the world this way. Provide a thorough description of the sociological imagination, then model its application. After you go through several examples, pose a problem to the class and have them try to analyze it using their best sociological imaginations. This can be done in small groups or with the class as a whole, depending on your situation and preference. Work through the problem with students, and they will gain confidence in its use.

3. **Sociology vs. Common Sense, Part 1.** There are essentially two kinds of "common sense" approaches to understanding society and social life. The first is exemplified in proverbs, as Tischler notes. What students need to understand is that this kind of common sense, though true on its own terms, doesn't always give them the *rules* or knowledge of the *governing conditions* for conflicting bits of folk wisdom. (for example, Is this a time when "the squeaky wheel gets the grease"? Or is it a time when "silence is golden"? Your job, your personal relationship — or your life — may depend on knowing the difference.) You can model this for students in a lecture, then ask them for examples. Usually they don't have much trouble thinking of them.

4. **Sociology vs. Common Sense, Part 2.** The other kind of "common sense" consists of the taken-for-granted understandings that people have about the social world — understandings that are often limited, misperceived, or plain wrong. You can get students thinking about this by reading a series of statements summarizing important research findings that relate to topics you will cover during the course of the

term. Only don't tell students that these are research findings. Simply say that you will read some statements and then want a class vote on whether they are true or false. The statements should all be phrased so that they are false. (for example, "Today's working husbands do about as much housework as their working wives." "The amount of money a school district spends on facilities and equipment significantly influences academic achievement." "Average African American family income has caught up to average white family income." NOT!!!) After you tell the students that all the statements were false, note the fact that some of them are having a visceral reaction against what you just said. After all, they *know* better. They have some personal experience or anecdote which *proves* that you and the rest of those sociologist types are *wrong!* Acknowledging this emotional reaction right up front can (1) give students permission to acknowledge their emotional reactions all through the course (and they *will* have them!) (2) give you the opportunity to stress that acquiring a sociological understanding of the world can make us uncomfortable it is true, but it is always better to know then not to know. If we know what's what, we have a chance of dealing with it. If we are governed by illusion and misinformation, we have only a random chance of being effective.

5. **Sociology, Religion, and Science.** These days it seems that an increasingly vocal minority of students are not interested in exploring society and social issues with an open mind. Their religious ideology answers all important questions. This issue is likely to come up as soon as you begin discussing science (for example, evolution vs. "creation science"). So why not launch a preemptive strike by discussing myth, logic, and science as various different ways of understanding and living in the world. They are each valid for their own purposes and in their own way. It is not a question of religion *vs.* science; the two are not incompatible, just different. I use the following story to illustrate the point. Just living in the world, you can believe anything you want about how and why it works the way it does. At the level of existing in the world, many beliefs are valid. For instance, if I am an auto mechanic and you believe that the reason your car runs is that there is an armadillo on a treadmill under the hood, who can best drive their car? The answer is both. The car works the same for either of us — when we turn the key, it runs, regardless of our beliefs. But what if it doesn't run? Who has a better chance of repairing it — you with your Armadillo Chow, or me with my *Chilton's* manual? So it's only when we want to *affect* the workings of the world that we need to have science.

6. **Sociology as a Social Science.** When they analyze the social world, most students rely almost exclusively on personal experience and anecdotal evidence. One of the goals here is to get them to look at patterns and think about what constitutes scientific evidence. Here is an amusing way of challenging their taken-for-granted notions. I collect headlines from the tabloid newspapers available in grocery store checklanes. I then read examples of this "news" (the more outrageous the better!) to students. Of course they laugh and dismiss most of it out of hand. (You may want to ask for some of their personal favorites, too!) But then I ask then *why* they feel they can do this. After all, how do they *really know* that this stuff is any less true than what they read in so-called "legitimate" newspapers or magazines? What criteria can we use for separating the proverbial wheat from the chaff? Without really realizing it, students have begun to think about the criteria for science. And they have also seen how this is *not* an idle issue — it relates immediately and directly to their lives.

7. **Science and Fuzzy Logic.** The scientific approach known as "fuzzy logic" asserts that the world (and therefore the science necessary to understand it) is nonlinear, multivalent, and contradictory. Things exist and are true to a matter of degree. An excellent, accessible book on this is Bart Kosko's *Fuzzy Thinking* (see Resources). As does Kosko, you can have a lot of fun with examples of fuzzy thinking. For example: Write on the board, put up on an overhead, or wear a badge that says "Don't Trust Me." (Well? Should students trust your statement — or you — or not???) Is someone who is 30 old? Obviously, they are both old and not old to a degree. This is not a matter that can be resolved with finality by a single answer. Kosko's book is an excellent source of examples from the natural world that

we social scientists can use to show students that sociology is no less a science despite all its qualifications and cautions regarding interpretation of data. It turns out that the natural world is fuzzy, too!

8. **Science, Empiricism, and Paradigms.** Tischler observes that science relies on empirical evidence. Later in this chapter he introduces the concept of paradigm, or a way of interpreting evidence and guiding research. While it is important to get students to see the advantage and importance of empirical evidence, we don't want to have them make a fetish of it. Empirical evidence must still be *interpreted;* that is, we must use our interpretative faculties to make sense of the evidence of our senses. A wonderful resource for raising questions and generating examples on this issue is Philip and Phylis Morrison's PBS series *The Ring of Truth* and book by the same name (see Resources at the end of this chapter). You might want to show a segment of the video, or just use examples from the book (for example, how come we can never catch up to the "wet spot" on the pavement on a sunny summer day? What happens when a magician pulls a rabbit out of a hat?)

9. **Sociology's Founders and the Sociology of Knowledge.** It helps students to better understand and remember the classical theorists if you provide a little more background on them. You might want to tell students about the social conditions at the time each theorist was writing, as well as relate the theorist's personal biography and how their ideas were received. A good resource for doing this is Lewis Coser's theory book (see Resources at the end of this chapter). What we want to avoid, I think, is the "great man" view of history. On the one hand, we want to demonstrate the use of the sociological imagination to students by embedding the classical theorists in their respective social contexts and showing that individuals alone do not make history. On the other hand, we want to avoid giving the impression that only men have thought important thoughts about society (see next item).

10. **Sociology's Founders, Part 2: Gender, Race, and Class Bias.** In this edition, Tischler has added material on Harriet Martineau and a box on important early contributions by women to the development of sociology. A good additional resource may be found in the works of Dale Spender (see Resources section). In addition, we must recognize that sociology arose in Europe during a period in which it was assumed that European society and thought had risen to a plateau higher than (and therefor superior to) any previous or existing civilization. An excellent corrective to this bias is found in Samir Amin's *Eurocentrism* (See Resources). A good example of the role that racism played in the construction of social theory and history in the 19th century is Martin Bernal's massive and controversial study, *Black Athena* (See Resources). While you cannot assign this work to introductory students, you can obtain from it some interesting examples of intellectual bias to discuss in class. A video has been made about the controversy; check your sources to see if it is available. (I got a copy from our university library.) You might also want to ask your class why none of sociology's founders came from the working class, and how would sociology be different if they had had such origins? If you'd like some sociological analysis from the point of view of someone with working-class origins who became a professional sociologist, check out Robert Schrank's *Ten Thousand Working Days* (see Resources). Schrank describes and analyzes his work life, from menial labor to a sociologist with the Ford Foundation, never losing sight of, nor respect for, his working-class milieu. The book is insightful, humorous, and highly readable.

11. **Sociology, Individualism, and Freedom.** Individualism and freedom are important ideas that emerged from the Enlightenment and since that time have powerfully influenced economics, politics, and culture in Western Europe and North America. We must be careful, once again, not to be Eurocentric and assume that something must be wrong with the rest of the world for not developing these concepts in similar fashion (or not listening to us when we tell them to adopt our versions). A good antidote to this view is Orlando Patterson's excellent book, *Freedom* (see Resources). Patterson suggests that the

appropriate question is not "Why didn't the concept of freedom develop in the rest of the world?" but rather "Why did it happen to develop *only* in Western Europe?" Tischler discusses Patterson's ideas briefly in a box in Chapter 9 of the text. Getting students to think about Patterson's argument early in the course is a good way to get them exercising their sociological imaginations.

12. **Theoretical Perspectives.** Briefly discuss some examples of research from each perspective. If you select studies for their relevance and appeal to students, you can demonstrate that these perspectives are alive and useful.

13. **Theory and Practice.** If possible, invite colleagues into your class to briefly talk about their work — but only on a conversational level that the students can relate to. If you can get your colleagues to talk about why they do what they do, and what theory informs their work, the ideas of both theory and research will be personalized for the students, and they will get the idea, right at the beginning of the introductory course, that a variety of people, with a variety of views, do this kind of work. This can be important, not only for the content of the course, but to get some of the students thinking about sociology as a possible career.

SUGGESTED ACTIVITIES

1. **Introductions.** Having students introduce themselves early in the course is a significant way to validate the importance of each student, recognize the diversity of people and experiences present in the classroom, and create an atmosphere of informality and mutual respect. Nametags or desk tags (folded-over index cards) are not out of line if a goal of yours is getting students to interact with one another. There are a variety of ways to handle introductions. One way is to pair students up, give them a short while to talk with each other, then have each student introduce *their partner* to the class as a whole. This forces students to learn something about someone else. Since everyone's doing it, though, it's usually non-threatening. And a lot of interesting information usually comes out because as individuals we don't entirely control what seems interesting about us to another person. By commenting on each introduction, noting similarities and validating differences, you as the instructor can do much to create a positive atmosphere for the class. You can also draw out and/or announce a variety of sociological themes that arise from student stories.

2. **More on Introductions.** Another way to have students introduce themselves, one that is perhaps more revealing (and therefore more threatening to some) and also more likely to evoke sociological themes, is to have students do the "Who Am I?" exercise. A well-known social psychology experiment and diagnostic counseling technique, this exercise appears in the Study Guide for Chapter 4. It involves writing Who Am I? at the top of a blank sheet of paper, numbering 1 to 20 down the left-hand side (you may want to cut it to 12-15 to save time here), and then providing that many answers to the question. You can have students exchange papers (that's the threatening part!) and have the partner introduce the person. As students conduct the introductions, it gives you the opportunity to preview many themes that will be covered in the course: status and role, ascribed vs. achieved status, personality traits and socialization, the social definition of race and ethnicity, various definitions of social class, the self-fulfilling prophecy, etc. This should pique students' interest and draw them into the class by showing them that much of what you're going to cover has relevance to understanding their lives.

3. **Sociologists vs. Journalists and Talk-Show Hosts.** Tape a segment of Donahue or Oprah or Geraldo or Sally Jesse (the wilder the better, probably!). Show the tape to the class, then divide them into groups to work out how a sociologist would analyze the same issue. You can also do this exercise by bringing in selected magazine or newspaper articles on social issues and having the students analyze them vis à vis

sociological approaches. Or, in another twist on this idea, have the students themselves bring in articles for analysis. (Show-and-tell, I've found, is just as popular with college students as it is with pre- and primary schoolers!) This gets the students noticing articles in their environment and beginning to look at them in a fresh (i.e., sociological) way.

4. **Sociology vs. Common Sense.** In Chapter 1, Tischler juxtaposes some conflicting proverbs. Ask the students to come up with their own opposing pairs. This could be done in class, or as a "homework" assignment. It gets the students thinking about "common sense" wisdom, where it comes from, and what it means.

5. **The Sociological Imagination.** Have students go to different public places (e.g., McDonald's, the mall, an airport) and observe behavior. Have them write up their findings, first as a journalist would, then as a sociologist. This can form the basis of an interesting class discussion. You could also ask students to think/write about how other types of social scientists would view the same phenomenon. How would their interpretations be different?

6. **Sociology and Other Social Sciences.** Pose a problem or series of social problems to the class and then ask them to describe how different types of social scientists would approach the problem. This can be done in groups or as a writing assignment.

7. **Sociology's Founders.** Divide the students into groups and have them research and then present to the class some background information on the classical theorists. But don't forget to include often-overlooked female — and possibly non-European — theorists (see Resources below).

8. **Manifest vs. Latent Functions.** Give the students examples of social institutions, organizations, roles, norms, etc. and ask them, in small groups, to come up with a list of manifest and latent functions. This can be very enlightening for them, as they begin to realize that things are not always what they seem.

RESOURCES FOR THE INSTRUCTOR

Samir Amin, *Eurocentrism.* New York: Monthly Review Press, 1989.

Martin Bernal, *Black Athena: The Afroasiatic Roots of Classical Civilization. Vol. I: The Fabrication of Ancient Greece 1785-1985.* New Brunswick, NJ: Rutgers University Press, 1987.

Lewis Coser, *Masters of Sociological Thought: Ideas in Historical and Social Context, 2nd ed.* New York: Harcourt Brace Jovanovich, 1977.

Bart Kosko, *Fuzzy Thinking: The New Science of Fuzzy Logic.* New York: Hyperion, 1993.

Philip and Phylis Morrison, *The Ring of Truth: An Inquiry into How We Know What We Know.* New York: Random House, 1987.

Orlando Patterson, *Freedom: Freedom in the Making of Western Culture.* New York: Basic Books, 1991.

Dale Spender, *Women of Ideas, & What Men Have Done to Them.* London: Pandora Press, 1982.

Robert Schrank, *Ten Thousand Working Days.* Cambridge, Mass: MIT Press, 1978.

RESOURCES FOR THE STUDENT

Discovering Sociology

Zygmunt Bauman, *Thinking Sociologically.* Cambridge, Mass.: Basil Blackwell, 1990.
> A very personal introduction to the value of understanding sociology. The author's contention is that, at its best, sociology is exciting and subversive, and should serve the "cause of freedom." Bauman demonstrates just how sociology could do so by examining many of the pressing issues of contemporary life.

Peter L. Berger, *Invitation to Sociology: A Humanistic Perspective.* Garden City, NY: Doubleday Anchor Books, 1963.
> A timeless classic, in which readers are invited in a friendly way to go along on the sociological voyage of discovery.

Lewis A. Coser (ed.), *The Pleasures of Sociology.* New York: New American Library, 1980.
> A collection of 36 highly readable essays by outstanding sociologists that show the field at its most insightful and intriguing best.

Anthony Giddens, *Sociology: A Brief But Critical Introduction, Second Edition.* San Diego: Harcourt Brace Jovanovich, 1987.
> A brief introduction to the field by one of the most important contemporary sociological theorists. This book is unique in that its approach is theoretical, historical, and comparative.

C. Wright Mills, *The Sociological Imagination.* New York: Oxford University Press, 1959.
> Some of this book is a bit dated, but much of it remains a lively critique of the field, and the first chapter, entitled "The Promise," is still by far the best description of the sociological imagination.

The Classical Theorists

Randall Collins and Michael Makowsky, *The Discovery of Society, 2nd edition.* New York: Random House, 1978.
> Profiles over a dozen classical theorists in an approach that provides excellent social and historical context as well as comparison and contrast among the thinkers. Brief and well-written.

Lewis A. Coser, *Masters of Sociological Thought: Ideas in Historical and Social Context, 2nd edition.* New York: Harcourt Brace Jovanovich, 1977.
> Provides a fairly comprehensive social, intellectual, and personal biographical context for about 15 major sociological theorists.

The Tavistock *Key Sociologists* series (London: Tavistock).
> Brief but sophisticated introductions to the historical and intellectual context and main ideas of many social thinkers. Series includes, among others, *Max Weber* (F. Parkin), *Émile Durkheim*(K. Thompson), and *Marx and Marxism*(P. Worsley), all copyright 1982.

Jonathan H. Turner, *Herbert Spencer: A Renewed Appreciation.* Beverly Hills, CA: Sage Publications, 1985.
> An attempt to recognize Spencer's pioneering contributions as well as show their relevance to today.

Contemporary Sociology

R.P. Cuzzort and E.P. King, *Twentieth-Century Social Thought, 4th edition.* Fort Worth: Holt, 1989.
> A highly-readable survey of 13 major contemporary theorists, including G.H. Mead, Merton, Mills, Goffman, and Garfinkel.

SOCIOLOGY = The scientific study of human society and social interactions.

The <u>*scientific*</u>$_1$ study of <u>*human*</u>$_2$ <u>*society*</u>$_3$ and <u>*social interactions*</u>$_4$.

1 *SCIENTIFIC* ⇨⇨⇨ <u>SCIENCE</u> = Logical, systematic methods of empirical investigation *and* the knowledge thereby obtained.

2 <u>HUMAN</u> = To be human is to be fundamentally *social* and *symbolic*.

3 *SOCIETY* ⇨⇨⇨ <u>PATTERNS</u> = The observed regularities of social life.

4 *SOCIAL INTERACTIONS* ⇨⇨⇨ <u>GROUPS</u> = Sets of people who interact on the basis of shared expectations.

<u>*SOCIOLOGY'S BASIC INSIGHT:*</u>

Human behavior is largely shaped by the groups to which people belong.

CHAPTER TWO: Doing Sociology: Research Methods

CHAPTER OUTLINE

The Research Process
> Define the Problem
> Review Previous Research
> Develop One or More Hypotheses
> Determine the Research Design
> > Surveys
> > Participant Observation
> > Experiments
> Define the Sample and Collect Data
> > Researcher Bias
> Analyze the Data and Draw Conclusions
> Prepare the Research Report

Objectivity in Sociological Research
> *Taking the Sociological Perspective: How to Read a Table*

Ethical Issues in Sociological Research
> Research Fraud
> *Controversies in Sociology: How Much Faith Should We Put in Political Polls?*

LEARNING OBJECTIVES

1. Explain the steps in the sociological research process.

2. Translate questions into testable hypotheses.

3. Identify independent and dependent variables in statements of causation.

4. Analyze the strengths and weaknesses of the various research designs.

5. Explain the process of sampling and evaluate the representativeness of samples.

6. Recognize researcher bias and explain how it can affect the outcome of research studies.

7. Explain the strengths and weaknesses of the various measures of central tendency.

8. Read a table and appropriately interpret its contents.

9. Explain the concepts of reliability and validity in sociological research.

10. Describe the problems of objectivity and ethical issues that arise in sociological research.

KEY CONCEPTS

The Research Process

research process: a sequence of steps that is followed when designing and carrying out a research project.

empirical question: a question that can be answered by observing and analyzing the world as it is known.

operational definition: a specific statement about an abstract concept in terms of the observable features that describe the thing being investigated.

hypothesis: a testable statement about the relationships between two or more empirical variables.

variable: any factor that can change or take on different values.

statement of causality: a declaration that some factor brings about, influences, or changes something else.

statement of association: a declaration that changes in one thing are related to changes in another, but that one does not necessarily bring about or induce changes in the other.

dependent variable: a factor that changes in response to changes in the independent variable.

independent variable: a factor that changes for reasons that have nothing to do with the dependent variable.

survey: a research method in which a population, or a portion thereof, is questioned to reveal specific facts about itself.

cross-sectional study: an examination of a population at a given point in time.

longitudinal study: research that investigates a population over a period of time.

interview: a conversation between two (or occasionally more) individuals in which one party attempts to gain information from the other(s) by asking questions.

structured interview: a form of research conversation in which a questionnaire is followed rigidly.

semistructured interview: a form of research conversation in which the investigator is free to vary the questions or even to make up new ones if the situation warrants.

participant observation: researchers enter into a group's activities as a method for investigating the group.

experiment: research based upon precise observation and measurement and extensive control of the variables being studied.

sample: the particular subset of the population chosen for study.

sampling: a technique in which researchers study a manageable subset of people selected from the population under study.

representative sample: a subset of the population that exhibits, in equivalent proportion, the significant variables that characterize the population as a whole.

sampling error: the result of failing to achieve a representative sample.

random sample: method of selecting subjects so that each individual in the population has an equal chance of being chosen.

stratified random sample: a method used to prevent certain groups from being under- or over-represented in a sample.

researcher bias: the tendency for researchers to select data that support, and to ignore data that seem to go against, their hypotheses.

blind investigators: investigators who do not know whether a specific subject belongs to the group of actual cases being investigated or to a comparison group.

double-blind investigators: investigators who are kept uninformed not only of the kinds of subjects they are studying but also of the hypotheses being tested.

analysis: the process through which large and complicated collections of scientific data are organized so that comparisons can be made and conclusions drawn.

validity: the extent to which a study tests what it was intended to test.

reliability: the characteristic of a study that indicates that the findings are repeatable.

LECTURE SUGGESTIONS

1. **The Research Process.** Choose a research study with which you are familiar — one that will appeal to students — and follow it through each of the steps of the research process. You may want to construct a flowchart to emphasis the decisions and tradeoffs that are made at each step of the process. A handout that I use to reinforce the information on the research process may be found in the Resources section at the end of this chapter. It is important, I think, to convey to students the contingent nature of research. Too often, the presentation of findings in textbooks hides the process from students and makes it all seem cut-and-dried. Disabusing students of this notion can both reduce the awe in which they have been taught to hold science and, paradoxically, to generate more respect for the undertaking. An excellent source for insights, examples, and references regarding the research process is Delbert Miller's *Handbook of Research Design and Social Measurement* (see Resources at the end of this chapter).

2. **Students and the Research Process.** After you have modeled the process for students, see if they can do it. Have the class agree on a particular problem they want to know more about. Then have them generate hypotheses, think about measurement and research design, etc. (This can be done in small groups, too.)

3. **Sociologists as Detectives.** Tischler suggests near the beginning of this chapter that sociological research and detective work have a lot in common. Use this metaphor to model the research process. You may want to draw explicitly on famous detectives from literature, film, or television. Not only does this make for a lively class, but it connects sociological knowledge to things the students already know — a proven effective teaching and learning technique.

4. **Item Validity.** Make students aware of the biases that can be built into questions, especially on surveys — too vague, too difficult, too sensitive, too confusing, easily misinterpreted, socially-appropriate answers, etc. The best way to do this is to provide them with examples (preferably drawn from popular research), then see if they can generate some examples on their own.

5. **More on Item Validity: Course Exams and Essays.** Every student has a horror story about an exam question or essay assignment that was absurdly off target. You could ask students to share some of these stories in class (without identifying the instructors!). After all, we know that students enjoy complaining! Even better, have students try to write questions for your own course material (essay and multiple-choice). This could be done in small groups or as a writing assignment. It might give students a feel for problems of validity. Alternatively, you could have students write questions for a campus opinion poll, then have them peer critique the validity of the questions.

6. **Researcher Bias.** Discuss the phenomenon of the self-fulfilling prophecy, showing both how it introduces biases into research and how it can be controlled for through techniques like random selection and blind and double-blind investigations. Pose situations to the class in which a researcher's objectivity may potentially be compromised — even for laudable reasons (e.g., wanting desperately to find a cure for AIDS, desiring to find a magnitude and seriousness in the problem of homelessness such that politicians will be forced to take action, etc.).

7. **Measures of Central Tendency.** Students are used to seeing distributions described by the mean or average; they are less accustomed to seeing the median. Yet it is important that they understand the strengths and weaknesses of each, and how they are often more powerful descriptors when used in tandem. Make sure that, whenever you return graded assignments or exams, you discuss the distribution of grades and measures of central tendency. By applying these concepts to something highly relevant to the students ("How did everyone else do on this assignment/test?") you not only help them understand the concepts, but you give them practical skills they can use elsewhere.

8. **Bias in Measures of Central Tendency.** One common form of bias in the popular presentation of measures of central tendency relates to income data. Since income is rarely distributed normally (i.e., on a normal curve), citing "average" or "per capita" income (which is the same thing) can be highly deceptive. I use this simple example in class (a variation on an exercise in the Study Guide). Suppose I told you that I know five people whose average income is $220,000. What would you think about their income? (Obviously, it's high.) I then write the following five incomes on the board: $1,000,000, $40,000, $30,000, $20,000, $10,000. Any student with a calculator or a quick mathematical mind can quickly verify that the mean of these five incomes is $220,000). I then ask: "What is the *median* income of this group?" ($30,000) "Which measure — mean or median — is a more accurate descriptor of this distribution?" In this way, students become aware of how extreme scores can skew the average. They need to be aware of this since nearly all popular presentations of income figures use the average (or per capita, which is the same thing). (Sometimes writers call it that even when it's really the median!) Just knowing this, students will be more educated consumers of statistics.

9. **Statistical Presentation and Deception.** Many students have in their minds a distorted view of Mark Twain's famous dictum, "Not all figures lie, but all liars figure." They tend to feel that all statistics, at some level, "lie." That is, you can make statistics say anything you want. Taken further, the conclusion is that no statistics are really valid. I think that we should confront this misperception directly by giving students examples of both inappropriate and appropriate use of statistics. Two good source of information and examples for this purpose are Hans Zeisel's classic, *Say It With Figures* and Richard Jaeger's *Statistics: A Spectator Sport* (see Resources).

10. **Ethical Issues in Research.** Pose some ethical dilemmas in research to the class; it usually is not hard to get a lively discussion going on this issue. Laud Humphrey's famous study, described in the Study Guide, is always a good bet. Also, you may want to talk about the problem of reactive effects and efforts to research humans in a naturalistic setting. Given that the technology of "snooping" is highly advanced today, how far can we justifiably go in invading people's privacy, even in public places? Even when this

invasion generates highly reliable data about people's social behavior?

SUGGESTED ACTIVITIES

1. **Decoding Popular Presentations of Research.** Find relatively detailed presentations of social research findings in newspapers and magazines. (This isn't always that easy to do! Opinion poll results are usually a readily available example, though.) Copy and pass this information out to the class after you have covered the research process. Then have the students go through it (collectively, in small groups, or individually as a writing assignment) and assess the strengths and weaknesses of the research along each step of the process. This experience makes them far more critical consumers of social science data.

2. **Generating Hypotheses.** Prepare in advance a number of lists of variables that may indeed be related, but do not indicate that relationship — simply list the variables. In class, divide students into groups and give each group a list of variables. Ask them to generate hypotheses around this list. They should be encouraged to begin by brainstorming — no idea is too wild or far out to be listed. You might even want to encourage students to be a little wild. This usually gets their creative juices flowing and also provides a means for discussing with them that science is often advanced by those willing to entertain "wild" ideas.

3. **Evaluating Research Designs.** Pose a hypothesis to the students (or have them come up with one) and then, in small groups, have them discuss and write up how they would research the identical hypothesis using *each* of the three designs presented by Tischler (or four designs as presented in my handout — see Resources below). Note for them — if they don't notice it themselves — that some nuances of the hypothesis are more amenable to being investigated by some methods than others. Choice of design influences findings. This exercise should also give students a feel for the strengths and weakness of each research design.

4. **Representative Samples and Sampling Bias.** Bring in examples of research reported in newspapers and magazines. Copy and pass it out to students. Then ask them to evaluate (possibly as a writing assignment) the representativeness of the samples used. Be sure you have some reasonably good as well as trashy examples. In the class discussion, make sure that students become aware of the whole range of possible biases (e.g., response rates and reactive effects of mail vs. phone vs. in-person interviews etc.). Give students as many examples and as much practice as possible in evaluating samples and thinking about how to ensure randomness. Unless you bring this abstract concept down to a practical level, most students won't get it, and it is vital that they do if they are to be educated consumers of social science research.

5. **Reading Tables.** Copy one or more data tables of interest and hand them out to the class. Good sources of tables include the *Statistical Almanac of the U.S., Current Population Reports* from the U.S. Census, and *Monthly Labor Review,* which includes data on employment and income. As a writing assignment and/or in small groups, have the students analyze the data according to the criteria laid out by Tischler in the box in Chapter 2. Another possibility is to ask students to generate hypotheses that are capable of being tested with the data you have given them. This is a pretty sophisticated application of knowledge and skills. If you use table analysis as a writing assignment, it is a good candidate for peer critique. Have students read each other's papers and give feedback on whether the table is summarized and analyzed clearly and accurately. This provides an alternate method for learning and reinforcing the necessary skill of table reading.

RESOURCES FOR INSTRUCTORS

Richard M. Jaeger, *Statistics: A Spectator Sport, Second edition.* Newbury Park, CA: Sage, 1990.

Delbert C. Miller, *Handbook of Research Design and Social Measurement, Fifth edition.* Newbury Park, CA: Sage, 1991.

Hans Zeisel, *Say It With Figures, 6th ed.* New York: Harper & Row, 1985.

RESOURCES FOR STUDENTS

The Research Process

Earl R. Babbie, *Social Research for Consumers.* Belmont, CA: Wadsworth, 1982.
> One of the few research methods books available that specifically addresses itself to students as consumers of scientific research and data. Written in a very conversational style.

Lucy Horwitz and Lou Ferleger, *Statistics for Social Change.* Boston: South End Press, 1980.
> One of the best introductions to statistics, designed to be used for self-study, and written in a conversational style.

Paul D. Leedy, *How To Read Research and Understand It.* New York: Macmillan, 1981.
> A relatively brief paperback that systematically demystifies all aspects of the presentation of research findings.

Herman W. Smith, *Strategies of Social Research, 3rd edition.* Fort Worth: Holt, Rinehart and Winston, 1991.
> An up-to-date survey of research strategies that is very comprehensive in its coverage of different methods.

Objectivity in Sociological Research

William Foote Whyte, in collaboration with Kathleen King Whyte, *Learning From the Field: A Guide From Experience.* Beverly Hills, CA: Sage, 1984.
> A passionate argument for the overriding importance of an applied, reflexive social research approach. Written by a justly famous sociologist, based upon his experience as a pioneer in a number of fields of sociological research.

Ethical Issues in Sociological Research

Paul D. Reynolds, *Ethics and Social Science Research.* Englewood Cliffs, NJ: Prentice Hall, 1982.
> An introduction to the ethical dilemmas faced by social scientists when they do research. Includes possible solutions.

SUGGESTED HANDOUT ON SOCIAL RESEARCH METHODS

AIMS OF RESEARCH / CRITERIA OF EVALUATION:
Reliability = consistency (Has the finding been obtained more than once?)
Validity = appropriateness (Do the measures actually measure what they purport to measure?)

THE RESEARCH PROCESS
Methodology = a system of rules, principles, and procedures that guides scientific investigation.
Steps:

1) Define the Problem
No problem, no need to research.
value neutrality (values have no influence) vs. objectivity (recognize and control for bias)

2) Review previous research
Look for existing data, problems, failures and success of others in examining the same problem.

3) Formulate a Hypothesis
Hypothesis = a testable statement about the relationship between 2 or more empirical variables
— it is a tentative explanation or prediction about the variables
Variable = a factor that can take on different values (i.e., vary).
Dependent variable = the phenomenon under study — i.e., what is trying to be predicted or explained.
(Can have only 1 at a time.)
Independent variable(s) = factors that are hypothesized to have a connection to the dependent variable.
The independent variables are not themselves explained; thus they are "independent" of the current hypothesis. (Can have many at a time.)
Variables must be **operationalized**, or given **operational definitions** — i.e., stated in terms that allow them to be explicitly measured.

4) Determine the Research Design
SURVEY
Goal is to determine the distribution of a variable in a **population**.
Forms of surveys include **mail**, **telephone**, and **face-to-face**.
Questions may be **open-ended** or **close-ended** (fixed choice).

FIELD STUDY
Goal is to examine social interaction "in the field" — i.e., in the locations where it normally or usually happens.
Includes **observation** (no direct researcher involvement) as well as **participant observation** (researcher is involved in the interaction under study).

EXPERIMENT
Goal is to isolate the independent and dependent variables by **controlling** for the effects of all variables not under study.

41

DOCUMENTARY

Goal is to make use of existing documented evidence to test a hypothesis.

"Documents" include records, tapes, film, video as well as written material.

Often accomplished through **content analysis**.

Research Design	Major Strength	Major Weakness(es)
Survey	Generalizability	Validity, Expense
Field	Sensitive to nuances	Subjectivity, Reactive effects
Experiment	Control	Generalizability
Documentary	Expands available data	Reliability

5) **Define the Sample and Collect the Data**

Through **sampling**, a manageable number of subjects are selected from the population being studied.

In order to guarantee that the sample is **representative** (has the same distribution of characteristics as the population studied), it must be **random** — i.e., every member of the population must have an equal chance of being included in the sample.

Sometimes this is accomplished through the use of a **stratified random sample**, which guarantees that segments of the population are represented in appropriate proportions.

In collecting the data, watch for **reactive effects** (the effect of the researcher on the research) — also known as "**the Hawthorne effect**."

Ethical questions are paramount here: To what extent does the end (reliable and valid data) justify the means (invasion of people's privacy; physical and/or psychological risk to the subjects)?

6) **Analyze the Data and Draw Conclusions**

Use **statistics** to look for **statistical significance** (a mathematical statement of the probability that the result is not due to chance alone).

Common statistics include:

frequencies — rates or percentages

measures of central tendency — mean, median, mode

measures of variability — variance, standard deviation

measures of association — correlation

For comparison, statistics must be **standardized** (i.e., calculated on the same base).

Different forms of data analysis and presentation can lead to different conclusions.

Conclusions about the same data can differ. All data must be interpreted; it is *never* true that "the facts speak for themselves."

7) **Report the Results**

• to other professionals, so that the reliability and validity of the methodology can be checked, and so that other explanations can be offered and other insights can be gained.

• to the subjects of the research, as a form of compensation.

CHAPTER THREE: Culture

CHAPTER OUTLINE

The Concept of Culture
    Culture and Biology
    Culture Shock
    Ethnocentrism and Cultural Relativism

Components of Culture
    Material Culture
    Sociology at Work: William Rathje — The Garbage Project
    Nonmaterial Culture
    Cognitive Culture
    Language and Culture
    Controversies in Sociology: Is There a Language Instinct?

The Symbolic Nature of Culture
    Signs, Symbols, and Culture

Culture and Adaptation
    Culture as an Adaptive Mechanism
    Mechanisms of Cultural Change
    Cultural Lag
    Animals and Culture

Subcultures
    Types of Subcultures
        Ethnic Subcultures
        Occupational Subcultures
        Religious Subcultures
        Political Subcultures
        Geographic Subcultures
        Social Class Subcultures
        Deviant Subcultures

Universals of Culture
> The Division of Labor
> The Incest Taboo, Marriage, and the Family
> Rites of Passage
> Ideology

Culture and Individual Choice
> *Taking the Sociological Perspective: The Conflict Between Being a Researcher and a Human Being*

LEARNING OBJECTIVES

1. Identify the basic features of culture and explain how culture makes possible the variation in human societies.

2. Distinguish between ethnocentrism and cultural relativism.

3. Describe and identify examples of material and nonmaterial culture and explain the role each plays in everyday life.

4. Explain the way language shapes our perception and classification of objects in the world and in situations that we encounter.

5. Discuss the role of culture in enabling humans to adapt to their environment.

6. Explain the roles of innovation and diffusion in the process of cultural change.

7. Identify instances of cultural lag in contemporary American society.

8. Describe and evaluate contrasting arguments about whether animals have culture.

9. List and explain examples of various subcultures.

10. Describe cultural universals.

11. Discuss the impact of cultural influences on individual choice.

KEY CONCEPTS

The Concept of Culture

> *culture:* all that humans learn to do, to use, to produce, to know, and to believe as they grow to maturity and live out their lives in the social groups to which they belong.

> *culture shock:* the difficulty people have when encountering a culture that is substantially different from their own.

> *ethnocentrism:* making judgments about other cultures based on the customs and values of one's own culture.

cultural relativism: the recognition that cultures must be studied and understood on their own terms before valid comparisons can be made.

Components of Culture

material culture: human technology, or everything made and used by humans.

nonmaterial culture: the totality of knowledge, beliefs, values, and rules for appropriate behavior.

norms: rules of behavior that are agreed upon and shared within a culture and that prescribe limits of acceptable behavior.

mores: strongly held rules of behavior that usually have a moral connotation and are based on the central values of the culture.

folkways: rules of behavior that permit a wide degree of individual interpretation.

ideal norms: expectations of what people should do under perfect conditions.

real norms: rules of behavior expressed with qualifications and allowances for practical circumstances.

cognitive culture: a component of culture consisting of shared beliefs and knowledge of what the world is like — what is real and what is not, what is important and what is trivial.

values: a culture's notions of what is good and bad, desirable and undesirable.

selectivity: a process by which some aspects of the world are viewed as important while others are virtually neglected.

Sapir-Whorf hypothesis: the view that the language that people use determines their perception of reality.

The Symbolic Nature of Culture

symbol: anything that represents something else and carries a particular meaning recognized by members of a culture.

Culture and Adaptation

adaptation: the process by which humans adjust to changes in their environment.

specialization: the process of developing ways of doing things that work extremely well in a particular environment or set of circumstances.

generalized adaptability: the process of developing more complicated yet more flexible ways of doing things.

innovation: any new practice or tool that becomes widely accepted in a society.

cultural traits: items of a culture such as tools, materials used, beliefs, values, and typical ways of doing things.

diffusion: the movement of culture traits from one culture to another.

reformulation: the modification of a cultural trait so that it fits better in its new context.

cultural lag: the phenomenon through which new patterns of behavior emerge, even though they conflict with traditional values.

Subcultures

subculture: the distinctive lifestyles, values, norms, and beliefs of certain segments of the larger population within a society.

Universals of Culture

cultural universals: models or patterns that have developed in all cultures to resolve basic problems.

incest: sexual relations between family members.

taboo: the prohibition of a specific action.

rites of passage: standardized rituals marking major life transitions.

ideologies: strongly held beliefs and values.

LECTURE SUGGESTIONS

1. **Cultural Variation.** Many students come to our introductory sociology courses with a relatively narrow range of cultural experiences. It is important for us to show them that there are *many* ways of being human, and no single one of them is inherently better than another. One way to expose the class to other cultures is to show them one or more short films or videos. Don't be hesitant to use excerpts from documentaries or even feature films (e.g., the first part of *The Gods Must Be Crazy*). Another way to get students thinking about other cultural views is through literature. Look for short stories, excerpts from biographies and autobiographies, even persuasive pieces like speeches. Anthologies are good sources for this material, for example, *The Heath Anthology of American Literature* mentioned in the Introduction.

2. **Culture and Biology.** The relationship between culture and biology is obviously complex. Most introductory students see these two as separately existing categories and functions. Most sociologists, on the other hand, see culture as interpenetrating biology. The way I put it to my students is that "culture regulates, interprets, and channels biology." The point is that, because humans lack instinctual determinism, cultural practices must be invented to help us meet our needs. Examples of this abound. One that always impresses students is that humans are the only animal species that will *voluntarily* take poison. We have to work hard to fool other animals into eating poison; if they have the slightest hint something is wrong, they won't eat the food. They are, for the most part, protected by their instincts. Humans, on the other hand, lack these instincts and so will deliberately ingest harmful substances despite clear warnings against it — e.g., warning labels on cigarette packages, nutritionists' advice about fat-laden foods, etc. On the issue of nutrition, you can point out to students that *what* we as humans eat, *when* and *how* we eat it, is largely influenced by culture, not biology. Ask students to reflect on the importance of the symbolic presentation of food relative to our enjoyment of it. Usually a good class discussion can be generated around cultural similarities and differences in the preparation of food.

3. **Ethnocentrism and Cultural Relativism.** If you have access to an anthropologist or other social scientist who has done fieldwork in another culture, invite them to come in and share their experiences with the class. See if they have had an experience similar to Kenneth Good's, described in the "Taking the Sociological Perspective" box in this chapter. If you know of someone, but aren't able to get them to come to class, don't overlook the possibility of videotaping their reflections on their work. (This could also be a student project — to create a videotaped interview with someone who has done cross-cultural fieldwork.) Usually the story is so fascinating and/or foreign to most students that they are not put off by a "talking head" on TV.

4. **Ethnocentrism and Cultural Relativism II.** Many students may be uncomfortable with a pure cultural relativism — i.e., one that suggests that each culture's ideas and practices are valid in their own right and can neither be compared nor judged. Indeed, Tischler suggests in this chapter that sometimes judgments must be made about cultural practices. Aside from moral issues, can/should we be able to make judgments regarding particular cultural practices? How shall we do so without being ethnocentric? Here I think that the concept of basic human needs is valuable. (A definition of basic human needs and two reasons for using the concept may be found on my Basic Concepts handout on page 19 of this Instructor's Manual.) I suggest Maslow's Hierarchy of Needs as a tool for making assessments of cultural practices (see Resources). On the one hand, it can be a fairly objective concept. On the other hand, it, too, must be placed in culturally relative context. Leading the students through this topic gives them a sense of how difficult it is to make objective assessments of other people's culture, to say nothing of our own.

5. **Ethnocentrism and Cultural Relativism III.** Bring in two or more sets of research findings about the same culture that are different, or perhaps diametrically opposed in their conclusions. Describe the findings to students, or have them look at the research themselves. Ask them to speculate, in writing and/or class discussion, about how different researchers, looking at the same culture, could have reached such different conclusions. What does this say about cultural relativism and ethnocentrism? Suggestions for research studies: Margaret Mead's and Derek Freeman's study of natives of New Guinea; controversy surrounding the Tasaday, the so-called "cave people" of the Philippines. There are several video documentaries exploring the Tasaday controversy.

6. **Material Culture.** Students are not used to thinking of material objects as *symbolic* components of *culture*. By discussing various aspects of material culture, you can get them to see it in a new way. This can often be done in a humorous way. For instance, I ask students to tell me the difference between a soup spoon and a teaspoon. While a number of students can describe the differences in their physical shape, almost no one can say *why* they are shaped that way or, why, while a soup spoon is used almost exclusively for soup, a teaspoon is hardly ever used for tea; nor does it typically hold a teaspoon's measure of liquid. So why the name? Obviously, it's arbitrary, but shared. A resource for seeing the social aspects of technology is Lewis Mumford (see Resources). Some of Mumford's work appears in a critical anthology of short articles on technology called *Questioning Technology* (see Resources).

7. **Material and Nonmaterial Culture.** If you can, arrange for a mime to come into the class and do a short skit. An alternative is to show a film or video of a mime. Marcel Marceau has a wonderful series of short pantomimes called "The Art of Pantomime" that is available through a number of film distributors. Just a five-minute pantomime can suggest all sorts of questions to the class. How did they know what was happening? How were they able to impute the existence of other people and/or objects if they weren't really there? Why are there similarities and differences in people's interpretations? Would people in another culture, someplace else in the world, immediately understand this pantomime just like they did? If not, why not? Does the existence of similarities and differences tell us anything about the relationship between biology and culture?

8. **Ideal vs. Real Norms.** Any class discussion of this topic is one ripe with opportunities for humorous reinforcement of the important difference between the "official" expectations and what people actually do. Here are two that I have used: (1) speed limits — anyone who has been driving for any more than six weeks or so has exceeded the legal speed limit. In fact, on the freeway, if you drive the speed limit you are likely to (a) make other drivers mad, and (b) get run over by large semi trucks. (2) student behavior — how many students have skipped a class, studied less than they should have, faked a reference in a paper, made up an excuse to an instructor (how many grandmothers do some students actually have, anyway???), etc.

9. **Language and Culture.** Once learned, language becomes so taken-for-granted that it is hard for many students to remember that language is arbitrary. One way to illustrate the total arbitrariness of language is to discuss color names. While physiologists tell us that the average human eye is capable of distinguishing over *seven million* separate shades of color, it is obviously too overwhelming to cope with that level of complexity. (Can you imagine the size of the Crayola 7-million box??!!) So we collapse the continuous spectrum of visible light into manageable categories, whose meaning is generally shared. As an example, ask everyone in the room wearing blue to stand up. Note to the students that all (or nearly all) of them got it right, though the shades of blue worn by the people standing vary considerably. At the other extreme, because the names for colors are completely arbitrary, they can become confusing. Go to a paint store and get some paint chips with exotic names. Then, in class, hold up several and read off a color name. Challenge the students to tell you which chip is that color. (Examples I have found: anemone, potpourri, musk. I'm not even going to tell you what colors these really look like. You'll have to do your own research.) Alternatively, you can use the famous Crayola 64-crayon Assortment. While students might have more familiarity with this, it can still be daunting (e.g., bittersweet, thistle, cornflower). This exercise simultaneously illustrates that symbols are arbitrary, but that they have various overtones of meaning (which is why somebody gets paid big bucks to come up with these alluring names!).

10. **Sapir-Whorf Hypothesis.** If you are familiar with a language besides English, and/or have members of your class who are, or have a helpful colleague who speaks another language, provide some examples of concepts that have different meanings, or different nuances of meaning, or no direct equivalents in English. Ask the class to speculate on why this is so.

11. **Culture and Adaptation.** There are many good films and videos on human evolution that emphasize the processes of cultural adaptation, innovation, diffusion, and reformulation. Many of them are short, or lend themselves to editing. Check with anthropologist colleagues, or see the descriptions in the catalogues of major film distributors. *The Gods Must Be Crazy* is a good feature film for this purpose, not only because it is amusing and readily available, but because it shows how well-adapted the native culture is to the Kalahari desert region, and how maladapted is European material culture.

12. **Cultural Diffusion and Reformulation.** Most students are not aware of how much of American culture can be traced to Native Americans. From foods and medicines to important aspects of our political and economic systems, we owe a great debt to the Indians. A good source for examples is the companion books by Jack Weatherford (see Resources).

13. **Culture and Individual Choice.** In the suggested handout about the definition of sociology found in Chapter 1 of this Instructor's Manual, I quoted the suggestion that sociology's basic insight is that human behavior is largely shaped by the groups to which we belong. I also suggested there that many students, socialized to individualism, may strongly resist this point. This is a good time to return to the point and reinforce how much students have already learned about the role of social influence in their lives. What does it mean to "show their individualism" by dressing in the same styles and speaking the same slang as

other members of their subculture? Ask students to come up with examples of the most individualistic behavior imaginable, then show the social influences on it. Are most students aware, for instance, that women who live together and closely identify with one another tend to have their menstrual periods on the same schedule? Although medical science can't explain it, obviously some sociocultural force is influencing what is, after all, an extremely individual biological function. Other examples can be posed to the class, or you can ask them to generate a list.

SUGGESTED ACTIVITIES

1. **Cultural Variation and Cultural Relativism.** In order to give students a sympathetic feel for other cultures, ask them to do "cultural guidebook" presentations on a culture that is "foreign" to them. These brief presentations could in fact rely on sources such as travel guides, but the important thing is that they sympathetically present the customs of another culture, as well as emphasize the need to respect those customs.

2. **Culture Shock.** In small groups, have the students discuss culture shock. Some might be able to discuss personal experiences of it. All of the students can speak to contemporary cultural artifacts and practices that might (and perhaps do) cause culture shock for their grandparents. Ask students to speculate on ways in which they might experience culture shock in the future.

3. **Ethnocentrism and Cultural Relativism.** Have students role-play (as a writing assignment and/or in front of the class) someone in an indigenous culture being contacted by someone from a European culture — for example, an Indian at Jamestown or Plymouth Colony in the 1620s; a West African encountering European colonist/explorers in the 16th century; an Aztec confronting Cortès and his Spanish army in 1519; Pochantas accompanying John Smith back to England; etc. By "putting themselves in the place of the other" in a concrete way, students should get a feel for relativism.

4. **Material Culture.** Have students, in small groups, make a list of all the material culture present in the classroom. After brainstorming a list, they should try to come up with at least two possible meanings for each object. You'll probably run out of time, the exercise should help students to look at material objects in a new way — i.e., as part of culture, with symbolic meanings attached.

5. **Material Culture: Garbage in the Classroom.** Ask students to save and examine their trash, as requested in a Study Guide exercise for this chapter. Ask them to take photos of the trash in a way that doesn't personally identify anyone as previous owner of the trash, and bring the *photos* (*not* the trash itself!!) into class. Collect the pictures, shuffle them, and pass them out to students in groups. Have the groups examine the material culture in the photos and interpret its meaning. Try to move them beyond just identifying the personal characteristics of the trash's previous owner, to inferring conclusions about society and social structure.

6. **Norms and Culture.** Harold Garfinkel has shown us that one of the most reliable ways to discover the significance of a norm is to violate it. After discussing with students the ethics of norm violation and social experimentation, send them out to violate some simple and safe norms: e.g., sitting in the "wrong" location at a library or cafeteria table when it is partially occupied; standing "too close" to someone waiting in a public hallway. Have them write up reports and share them in small groups and with the class as a whole. Have the students work together to classify the seriousness of the norms violated and the differences in people's reactions.

7. **Folkways vs. Mores.** Have the students, in small groups, make lists of various public behaviors and classify those behaviors as folkways or mores. Note that age, gender, and/or subcultural differences may emerge in the perception of the seriousness of certain norms. Comment on these differences.

8. **Ideal vs. Real Norms.** One type of project or assignment that really hits home is to have the students compose a hypothetical "survival manual" for incoming (i.e., newly matriculated) college students. In it, your students should list what they consider the major ideal norms of college life. Then they should proceed to the real norms — i.e., what a person can reasonably "get away with." Done as individual or group projects, this exercise is not only valuable for reinforcing the concept, but it is often extremely enlightening to the instructor!

9. **Cognitive Culture.** You may want to illustrate this concept by having students draw their own cognitive maps — of the campus, the town in which your college or university is located, etc. Students may then compare differences and speculate on the reasons for them in small groups. Alternatively, you may ask students in small groups to map a hierarchy of American values, and to discuss differences of opinion as related to subcultures.

10. **Cultural Innovation.** Select a cultural innovation (the railroad, the auto, mass public education, computers, etc.) and have students write and/or discuss how that innovation has affected American society, both for better and for worse.

11. **Animals and Culture.** On the board or on an overhead transparency, write the question "Do animals have culture?" Then give students ten minutes to write their answer. At the end of that time, have them exchange papers with others in a small group and then discuss the answers. By the time you get to a whole-class discussion, students will be fairly uninhibited in giving answers. Collect the students' papers at the end of the discussion (no names). Reading through them later, you will gain insight into what students do and don't understand about culture.

12. **Subcultures.** Have students generate and then compare in small groups lists of the subcultures in which they participate. They may be surprised at the extensiveness of the lists. You may want to generate statistics on mean/median number of subcultures participated in by individuals. One set of subcultures not discussed by Tischler is leisure subcultures. As there are dozens (hundreds?) of these, you may want students to restrict their list to just this category. Ask students to think about how subcultures are reinforced — specialty magazines, catalogs, stores, meetings, conferences, expositions, etc.

13. **Cultural Universals.** An idea for a short research paper is to have students find, compare and contrast examples of each cultural universal from two distinct cultures. Finding sources should not be difficult, and the process of writing should get students to think systematically about the arbitrariness of culture.

RESOURCES FOR INSTRUCTORS

Abraham Maslow, *Motivation and Personality.* New York: Harper and Row, 1970.

Lewis Mumford, *Technics and Civilization.* New York: Harcourt Brace Jovanovich, 1962.

John Zerzan and Alice Carnes (eds.), *Questioning Technology: Tool, Toy or Tyrant?* Philadelphia: New Society Publishers, 1991.

Jack Weatherford, *Indian Givers: How the Indians of the Americas Transformed the World.* New York: Crown Publishers, 1988.

Jack Weatherford, *Native Roots: How the Indians Enriched America.* New York: Crown Publishers, 1991.

RESOURCES FOR STUDENTS

The Concept of Culture
Colin M. Turnbull, *The Forest People: A Study of the Pygmies of the Congo.* New York: Simon and Schuster, 1962.
> A classic, highly-readable ethnography of the BaMbuti people of the central African rainforest. A good way to get inside another culture and see it from their point of view.

Robert N. Bellah, Richard Madsen, William M. Sullivan, Ann Swidler, and Steven Tipton, *Habits of the Heart: Individualism and Commitment in American Life.* New York: Harper and Row, 1986.
> An exploration of American values, the work portrays the tension between individual achievement and a sense of community. The argument is illustrated throughout with excerpts from the many personal interviews the authors conducted.

Culture and Adaptation
Marvin Harris, *Cows, Pigs, Wars, and Witches: The Riddles of Culture.* New York: Vintage, 1974.
> A classic work in which Harris demonstrates that seemingly bizarre practices by other cultures have have rational and identifiable roots in economic necessity. Highly readable.

Marvin Harris, *Cannibals and Kings: The Origins of Cultures.* New York: Vintage, 1977.
> The author demonstrates that cultural practices such as cannibalism, warfare, and unequal social castes can be explained as adaptations to particular ecological conditions. Highly readable.

Subcultures
Elliot Liebow, *Tally's Corner.* Boston: Little Brown, 1967.
> A pioneering look at "idle" African American streetcorner men in Washington, D.C.

William M. Kephart and William W. Zellner, *Extraordinary Groups: An Examination of Unconventional Lifestyles, Fifth edition.* New York: St. Martin's, 1994.
> A sociological look at non-mainstream American cultures: Old Order Amish, Gypsies, Hasidim, the Father Divine movement, the Oneida Community, etc.

William W. Zellner, *Countercultures: A Sociological Analysis.* New York: St. Martin's Press, 1995.
> A look at deviant subcultures (skinheads, KKK, satanists, survivalists, scientologists and Moonies), based on firsthand observations and in-depth interviews with current and former members.

CHAPTER FOUR: Socialization and Development

CHAPTER OUTLINE

Becoming a Person: Biology and Culture

    Nature versus Nurture: A False Debate

    Sociobiology

    Deprivation and Development

        Extreme Childhood Deprivation

        Infants in Institutions

The Concept of Self

    Dimensions of Human Development

        Cognitive Development

        Moral Development

        Gender Identity

Theories of Development

    Charles Horton Cooley (1864-1929)

    George Herbert Mead (1863-1931)

    Sigmund Freud (1856–1939)

    Erik H. Erikson (1902–1994)

    Daniel Levinson (1920–1994)

Early Socialization in American Society

    The Family

    Controversies in Sociology: Is Day Care Harmful to Children?

    The School

    Peer Groups

    The Mass Media

    Sociology at Work: Socialization Messages in Music Videos

Adult Socialization

    Marriage and Responsibility

    Parenthood

    Career Development: Vocation and Identity

    Aging and Society

LEARNING OBJECTIVES

1. Discuss how biological inheritance and socialization contribute to the formation of personality.

2. Evaluate sociobiology as an explanation for human behavior.

3. Explain how extreme social deprivation affects early childhood development.

4. Distinguish between social identity and the self.

5. Identify the stages of cognitive and moral development.

6. Explain the basics of the symbolic interactionist view of the self developed by Cooley and Mead.

7. Describe Freud's view that the self is constantly in conflict.

8. Describe and critique Erikson's and Levinson's stage models of lifelong socialization.

9. Explain how family, schools, peer groups, and the mass media contribute to childhood socialization in American society.

10. Explain how adult socialization differs from primary socialization.

11. Explain resocialization and describe the types of resocialization required by marriage, parenthood, career development, and old age.

KEY CONCEPTS

Becoming a Person: Biology and Culture

socialization: the process of social interaction that teaches the child the intellectual, physical, and social skills needed to function as a member of society.

personality: the patterns of behavior and ways of thinking and feeling that are distinctive for each individual.

genes: inherited units of biological material.

instincts: biologically inherited patterns of complex behavior.

conditioning: the molding of behavior through repeated experiences linking a desired reaction with a particular object or event.

sociobiology: the discipline that uses biological principles to explain the behavior of social beings.

nurture: the entire socialization experience.

social attachments: having feelings for others and seeing evidence that others care for us.

affiliation: meaningful interaction with others.

The Concept of Self

statuses: culturally and socially defined positions.

social identity: the total of all the statuses that define an individual.

self: one's changing yet enduring personal identity.

sensorimotor stage: when an infant relies on touch and the manipulation of objects for information about the world.

preoperational stage: when a child learns that words can be symbols for objects.

operational stage: when a child learns to think with some logic and can understand and work with numbers, volume, shapes, and spatial relationships.

formal logical stage: when a child becomes capable of abstract, logical thought and can anticipate possible consequences of acts and decisions.

moral order: the shared view of right and wrong that exists in a society.

gender identity: an individual's view of themselves resulting from their sex

Theories of Development

looking-glass self: the notion that other people mirror back to us important aspects of our sense of self.

the "I": in Mead's view, the portion of the self that wishes to be active and spontaneous.

the "me": in Mead's view, the portion of the self that is made up of everything learned through the socialization process.

significant others: individuals who are most important to our development.

generalized others: the viewpoints, attitudes, and expectations of society as a whole or of a general community within it.

preparatory stage: in Mead's view, the point at which a child learns role expectations by imitating the behavior of others.

play stage: in Mead's view, the point at which a child formulates relatively simple role expectations.

game stage: in Mead's view, the point at which a child learns the general expectations, positions, and rules of society.

id: in Freudian theory, the part of the self that consists of inherited drives and instincts that are mostly unconscious.

libido: in Freudian theory, the erotic or sexual drive.

superego: in Freudian theory, the part of the self that is society's norms and values as learned primarily from our parents.

ego: in Freudian theory, the part of the self that looks for ways to adjust to social realities and to express the id's drives in a socially acceptable fashion.

Early Socialization in American Society

   peers: individuals who are social equals.

   mass media: impersonal means of transmitting information to great numbers of people in a short period of time.

Adult Socialization

   primary socialization: the process of mastering the basic information and skills required of members of a society.

   adult socialization: the process by which adults learn new statuses and roles.

   resocialization: a process of exposure to ideas or values that in one way or another conflict with what was learned in childhood.

   total institution: environments in which the participants are physically and socially isolated from the outside world.

KEY THINKERS/RESEARCHERS

   Charles Darwin: author of the pathbreaking work *On the Origin of Species,* which led to humans being seen as a species similar to all other animals.

   Ivan Pavlov: his experiments with dogs demonstrated that so-called instinctive behavior could be molded or, as he called it, conditioned.

   John B. Watson: experimented with conditioning humans through a series of repeated experiences linking a desired reaction with a particular object or event.

   Edward O. Wilson: a major advocate of sociobiology as an explanation of human behavior.

   Stephen Jay Gould: a critic of sociobiology, he argues for cultural determinism of human behavior.

   Harry F. Harlow: his experiments with rhesus monkeys dramatically illustrated the harmful effects of social deprivation during infancy.

   Jean Piaget: discovered that children move through predictable stages on their way to developing logical thought.

   Lawrence Kohlberg: suggested that moral thinking progresses through five or six distinct stages.

   Charles Horton Cooley: a symbolic interactionist who conceived of the development of the self as a three-stage process in which other people mirror back to us important qualities of the self.

   W.I. Thomas: author of the idea that if people "define situations as real, they are real in their consequences."

   George Herbert Mead: argued that the self develops in interaction with significant others, from whom we learn increasingiy sophisticated role expectations.

   Sigmund Freud: pioneered the view that the individual and society are enemies, and that the individual self therefore constantly experiences conflict.

Erik Erikson: suggested a view of lifelong human development in which individuals move through eight stages of crises in which different stresses and conflicts must be resolved.

Daniel Levinson: developed a stage model of age-related developmental periods in the adult life cycle.

Rosalind Barnett and Grace Baruch: suggested that Levinson's stage theory may not apply to women because women's roles involve varying life structures that are not so centrally tied to chronological age.

Alice Rossi: argued that developmental stage theorists may be mistaken and may have merely described the pattern of a particular generational cohort of men.

Erving Goffman: developed the concept of a total institution as an important location for resocialization.

LECTURE SUGGESTIONS

1. **Deprivation and Development.** If you can, arrange to show excerpts from François Truffaut's *The Wild Child* (the story of J-M Itard and Victor) or *The Miracle Worker* (either the version with Patty Duke and Anne Bancroft or the one with Patty Duke and Melissa Gilbert). These films dramatically illustrate, on the one hand, the negative consequences of deprivation of human contact and, on the other hand, the beneficial effect of the social bond. Other examples abound. Tischler discusses Kingsley Davis' report on Anna. In the same article Davis relates the story of Isabelle, which I believe is even more compelling in its illustration of the salutary effects of social attachments. If you pay attention to newspapers and magazines you can, unfortunately, find a number of local examples of child abuse and deprivation. Students are probably aware of the more dramatic of these cases (because they are widely reported and discussed), and using them as examples brings the point home to students.

2. **Deprivation and Development II.** Many scientific popularizers have taken the sociological insight about the importance of social attachments and developed it into a mystical notion of the necessity of "bonding" with an infant at birth (see the section on childbirth in a shopping mall bookstore). In order to have a psychologically healthy child, these "experts" suggest, bonding must occur immediately at birth. This of course is not true. Bonding at birth is for the benefit of the parents, not necessarily for the immediate benefit of the child. The experience of adopted children and parents is instructive here (as is the experience of Helen Keller). In many of the latter cases, bonding does not occur until later. Yet it can still be successful (although, in truth, there are horror stories here as well). Many adoptive parents and adults who were adopted as children are quite willing to talk about their experiences. You may have some of these people in your class. If not, or if they are uncomfortable speaking out, check to see if there is a local network of adoptive families. Often members will be happy to speak about issues of bonding. Otherwise, there are a number of good books which you can find in the library and present to the students.

3. **Cognitive, Social, and Emotional Development.** In the Resources section at the end of this chapter is a chart that attempts to combine Piaget's model of cognitive development in childhood with Mead's notion of the evolution of role-taking ability, and Erikson's ideas about the emotional conflicts that children face at each stage of development. You may want to share this or a similar chart with your students in order to give them an integrated view of the dimensions of childhood socialization. When presented to students, the chart can be liberally illustrated with examples of specific behaviors typical of children at

each stage. I have found that the behavior of young children is a fascinating subject for students, even those who are not themselves parents. You probably can't give (or solicit from students) too many examples on this topic. An excellent film on child development is *Childhood: The Enchanted Years.* In addition, there is the recent PBS series entitled *Childhood.*

4. **Moral Development.** Kohlberg's ideas are quite controversial, and you may want to discuss that controversy with your students. One issue concerns possible ethnocentrism. To what extent are his standards of moral reasoning biased toward individualistic Americans? (Remember the story of Ahmed's boat in Chapter 3.) Another issue is the gender bias inherent in the categorization. This issue is thoroughly dealt with by Kohlberg's former assistant, Carol Gilligan (see Resources), and you may find it useful to bring her arguments in as a counterpoint.

5. **Freud.** Most students are going to have at least a primitive — if not entirely correct — notion of Freud's ideas prior to enrolling in introductory sociology ("He said we do everything because of sex.") You can enrich the presentation of his ideas with examples of "Freudian slips" and dream analysis and Freud's ideas about the tension between the individual and society, expressed in repression.

6. **"Accelerated" Childhood Development.** There is no evidence that intensive systematic education at a very early age creates gifted or talented children. On the contrary, it is more likely to create tense, overly serious youngsters who miss out on the playful aspects of their childhood, with potentially serious consequences. This doesn't stop numerous children's product manufacturers and "educational consultants" from trying to peddle this idea, however. Peruse magazines aimed at middle-class baby-boomer parents for any number of egregious examples that can be brought into class.

7. **Appropriate Functions of Primary Caregivers.** In the Resources section at the end of this chapter is a handout I put together to emphasize the three major functions of caregivers during primary socialization, the most important tasks involved in each of those functions, and the benefits for the child of carrying out those tasks effectively. The chart is based on a wide range of child development literature. I say "primary caregivers" because it applies to full- or part-time day care providers, preschool and primary school teachers, foster parents, and older relatives — anyone in a position to significantly influence the developing child.

8. **Adult Development: Self-Actualization.** In the Resources section is a handout I put together to describe the characteristics of self-actualizing people, according to Abraham Maslow. I use this not only to talk about social development at this juncture, but later in the course to analyze the impact of institutions on individuals.

9. **Styles of Primary Socialization.** In the Resources section is a handout I put together on Styles of Primary Socialization. It emphasizes the shortcomings of both the authoritarian and the permissive model and the benefits of a participatory model. The participatory model is worth emphasizing because, in my experience, most students do not see any alternatives beyond the authoritarian and permissive models. Many parents (and potential parents) think that they must choose between the Scylla of incurring resentment by being tough with their kids (or perhaps even being accused of abuse), or the Charybdis of "going easy on them" and raising antisocial monsters. This view is, unfortunately, reinforced by much of the popular media. Fortunately, this third, more healthy alternative is available. The participatory model derives from the humanist child development literature. A good single source is Ewens, cited below. You may want to share this handout with the class then see if they can extrapolate costs and benefits and come up with examples of the different models.

10. **Resocialization and Total Institutions.** Basic training in the military is a good example of both of these concepts. You may want to show excerpts from Frederick Wiseman's *cinema verité* film *Basic Training.* Or perhaps you can invite as a guest speaker a drill sergeant to discuss the philosophy and mechanics of the process. Even if you don't have a military base nearby, you are likely to have some National Guard, Army Reserve, or ROTC people in the area.

11. **Career Development: Vocation and Identity.** Have a corporate recruiter or someone from your Placement Office come in and give a guest lecture on what recruiters look for when trying to match people and jobs. Form a panel consisting of one or more workers who have experienced unemployment, someone from the local unemployment office, and someone from a local social service agency that deals with problems of unemployed people. Or you may have a colleague on your campus who conducts or is familiar with the research on the human consequences of unemployment. Invite them in for a guest lecture. Students may also have valuable stories to share here.

SUGGESTED ACTIVITIES

1. **Biology, Culture, and Society.** If students haven't done the "Who Am I?" exercise in class (see Chapter 1 of this Instructor's Manual), or if they haven't completed it as part of their Study Guide exercises for this chapter, have them do it now. Then, per the Study Guide exercise, have them code each answer for biological inheritance or social influence. This provides a basis for discussing just how much of a social product each one of us is. Ask students to write and/or reflect on what part of their identity is an integral part of their self as they see it, and what parts are open to change based on the social situations in which they find themselves.

2. **Conditioned Behavior.** Assign students selected material from B.F. Skinner's *Walden Two* and/or have students role play and read aloud some brief section where the residents of Walden Two explain, to the amazement of their visitors, how social conditioning works in their utopian community. Skinner's work is important because, whether or not you agree with his behaviorist theory, he presents a positive, proactive argument for conditioning. Most students, given their lack of knowledge of social influences, see conditioning as a bad word or a negative phenomenon. Using Skinner provides a springboard to discuss the many ways in which our behavior is, in fact, socially conditioned.

3. **Sociobiology.** Assign students to teams and have them debate sociobiology vs. cultural determinism. The debate could be based on just the material in the text, or you could require students to do some research by way of preparation. Regardless of how you do it, the debate format forces students to come to grips with the material in a practical way, and to really think about what explanation makes the most sense to them.

4. **The Looking-Glass Self.** To illustrate this concept to students in a dramatic but practical way, you can play the following simulation game. Divide the class into two roughly equal groups. Half the class gets labels pinned to their backs (or hung with string around their necks, but facing backwards). Obviously you need to make these labels up in advance. The labels should consist of various social characteristics and personality traits (e.g., intelligent, witty, boring, odd, hostile, athletic, conceited, mysterious, etc.). The people with labels are not allowed to see their own label. The goal is to see if they can guess their label based upon the nature of others' interactions with them. The half of the class without labels should be told that their task is to interact with each labelled person on the basis of the label, but being careful not to give away the actual label. After the people with labels have their labels in place, everyone stands up and moves around the room, interacting as at a cocktail party. Generally the people without labels

should try to interact with the people who have labels, and vice versa. After an appropriate period of time (depending on the number of interactors), the "cocktail party" stops and each labelled person, without looking, states what they think their label is, and why. Then they get to see if they are correct. Debriefing and discussion should occur. How did the labelled people feel? Pay particular attention to those who were given negative labels. Do they feel resentment? hostility? Emphasize that it was only an exercise, and not meant to be permanent. What about the people without labels? What labels were easy and what labels were difficult to convey? Can labels be categorized by difficulty? What can be learned from this exercise about the process of labelling? To what extent does it illustrate W.I. Thomas's statement that situations defined as real are real in their consequences?

5. **Peer-Group Socialization.** Have students, in small groups, share experiences of peers influencing them, for good or ill, during adolescence. After sharing stories, what can they conclude about the process by which this influence occurs? What are the manifest and latent functions of peer influence? Pose a problem such as youth gang behavior, and ask students to write and/or talk about how it happens and how its negative aspects could be controlled using peer influence.

6. **The Mass Media and Primary Socialization.** Assign students to watch an hour of two of television oriented to children (e.g., Saturday mornings, late afternoons on weekdays). Using content analysis, what themes would they identify as dominant? Even better would be if students could watch the television shows with pre-adolescent children and talk about the content as they watch. Is it true that children either do not pay much attention or are more capable of filtering messages than many adults think? Discussing these projects in class not only gives students a chance to share the fruits of their sociological imaginations, but it also gives them a feel for the complexities of researching a topic like this.

RESOURCES FOR INSTRUCTORS AND STUDENTS

Arthur L. Caplan, ed., *The Sociobiology Debate*. New York: Harper and Row, 1978.
    A comprehensive look at the history and context of the emerging discipline of sociobiology, along with statements by both the leading contemporary advocates and critics.

William L. Ewens, *Becoming Free: The Struggle for Human Development*. Wilmington, Del.: Scholarly Resources, 1984.
    A thought-provoking look at human nature, the characteristics of human development, and the conditions necessary for human growth.

Carol Gilligan, *In a Different Voice: Psychological Theory and Women's Development*. Cambridge, MA: Harvard University Press, 1982.
    Gilligan was a teaching assistant for Lawrence Kohlberg who became critical of the male bias in his concept of moral development. This book presents an alternative view.

Lucien Malson, Wolf Children and the Problem of Human Nature. New York: Monthly Review Press, 1972.
    A thorough discussion of the nature of human nature in light of evidence about so-called wolf children. Includes a listing of all recorded cases of feral children and the complete diary of Jean-Marc-Gaspard Itard detailing his experiences with Victor, the Wild Boy of Aveyron.

Jean Piaget, *The Construction of Reality in the Child.* London: Routledge and Kegan Paul, 1950.
    An exposition of Piaget's symbolic interactionist theories of child development.

CHARACTERISTICS OF SELF-ACTUALIZING PEOPLE

Self-Actualization = realizing one's potentials to the fullest

1. **Openness to Experience**
    They are unafraid of the unknown. They have less need to impose in advance a rigid structure upon experience.
    Result: less anxiety, more flexibility (more ability to "roll with the punches"), and more efficient perception of self, self needs, <u>and</u> the developing situation (due to fewer personal blinders).

2. **Self-Confidence**
    They are not incapacitated by excessive guilt, anxiety, or fears of inadequacy.
    Result: They do not waste their energies in unnecessary concern for the approval of others, or in seeking to avoid other people's disapproval or rejection.

3. **Sincerity**
    They most often act on the basis of their own principles and perceived needs, rather than on the basis of facades and pretended selves. Their interactions are characterized by honesty, candidness, genuineness, transparency, authenticity.
    Result: personal experience, personal awareness and interpersonal communication tend to be congruent (i.e., in harmony). No need to hide behind defenses.

4. **Integration**
    There is an internal interrelation between their intellect and their emotions.
    Result: Potentially "unacceptable" thoughts and feelings are not "disowned" or denied, but examined and come to terms with. Simplistic dichotomies and polarities are unneeded and therefore dissolved.

5. **Ability to Love**
    They have the capacity for forming deeper, more uninhibited intimate relationships with others. The main issue for them is not *being loved* by someone, but rather developing one's *capacity to love others.*
    Result: Greater capacities for empathy and mutual dialogue (better talkers *and* listeners), and a richer and far more satisfying sex life.

6. **Democratic Character Structure**
    They emphasize two-way dialogue and negotiated problem solving (win/win). They do not power- or status-trip others. They are willing to learn from anyone of suitable character.
    Result: Able to get along with many varieties of people. No evidence of sadomasochism in interpersonal relations.

FUNCTIONS OF PRIMARY CAREGIVERS FOR CHILDREN

1. Architect of the Child's World

Task of the Caregivers
- create a safe, accessible, stimulating environment
- introduce challenges appropriately

Benefits for the Child
- encourages curiosity and creativity
- develops self-esteem (sense of mastery/competence)

2. Consultant

Task of the Caregivers
- teach and explain about the physical and social worlds
- respond appropriately to excitement, frustration, pain
- give help when needed (and <u>asked</u>)

Benefits for the Child
- reinforces curiosity and the excitement of learning
- develops problem-solving abilities
- becomes confident and self-reliant, but aware of limitations
- learns to trust and rely on other people

3. Authority

Task of the Caregivers
- develop clear expectations; set limits
- respond consistently to child's behavior
- reward and punish appropriately

Benefits for the Child
- learns to take responsibility for her/his own actions
- develops self-esteem
- develops internal social control
- develops awareness of and sensitivity to the needs of others

STAGES OF PRIMARY SOCIALIZATION

AGE (Approx.)	SOCIAL DEVELOPMENT — Role-Taking Ability — G. H. Mead	SYMBOLIC DEVELOPMENT — Cognitive Abilities — Jean Piaget	EMOTIONAL DEVELOPMENT — Primary Emotional Conflicts — Erik Erikson
0 - 2	EGOCENTRIC	SENSORIMOTOR	TRUST vs. MISTRUST
2 - 5	IMITATION	← PREOPERATIONAL →	AUTONOMY vs. DEPENDENCY / INITIATIVE vs. GUILT
5 - 7	PLAY		
7 - 12	GAME	CONCRETE OPERATIONAL	← INDUSTRY vs. INFERIORITY →
12 +	THE GENERALIZED OTHER	FORMAL OPERATIONAL	IDENTITY vs. ROLE CONFUSION

Styles of Primary Socialization

	AUTHORITARIAN	PERMISSIVE	PARTICIPATORY
BASIC PREMISE	Children must be molded to conform to society	Children should not have their individual impulses restrained	Children need the freedom to explore and develop their own unique potentials
FOCUS	Adult-Centered — Needs of adults come first	Child-Directed — Children are demanding and nearly always win	Child-Centered — Oriented to child's needs, but *negotiated* with the needs of others
GUIDING PRINCIPLE	Obedience to Adults	Freedom from Restraint / Convenience	Freedom to Explore / Negotiated Limits
DISCIPLINE ORIENTATION	Strict — Narrow limits of acceptable behavior	Tolerant / Inconsistent	Supportive — No threatened love withdrawal
FAVORED SANCTION	Punishment	Absence of any / Inconsistent punishment	Rewards
OUTCOME	Inflexible people who lack curiosity and creativity	Manipulators with poor internal social control, low self-esteem, and anxiety about being loved	Creative people with high self-esteem, internal social control, and identification with others

CHAPTER FIVE: Social Interaction and Social Groups

CHAPTER OUTLINE

Understanding Social Interaction

Contexts

Norms

Taking the Sociological Perspective: Social Interaction in the Amish Community

Types of Social Interaction

Nonverbal Behavior

Exchange

Cooperation

Conflict

Competition

Elements of Social Interaction

Statuses

Roles

Role Sets

Role Strain

Role Conflict

Role Playing

The Nature of Groups

Primary and Secondary Groups

Functions of Groups

Defining Boundaries

Choosing Leaders

Making Decisions

Setting Goals

Assigning Tasks

Controlling Members' Behavior

Reference Groups

Small Groups

Large Groups: Associations
>   Formal Structure
>   Informal Structure

Bureaucracy
>   Weber's Model of Bureaucracy: An Ideal Type
>   Bureaucracy Today: The Reality
>   The Iron Law of Oligarchy

Institutions and Social Organization
>   Social Institutions
>   Social Organization
>   *Controversies in Sociology: Can We Control Trial Outcomes Through Jury Manipulation?*

LEARNING OBJECTIVES

1. Explain the pervasiveness of social interaction among humans.

2. Explain how contexts and norms influence social interaction.

3. Describe and illustrate major types of social interaction.

4. Describe and illustrate the concepts of status and role.

5. Identify the major characteristics of social groups and differentiate groups from social aggregates.

6. Distinguish between primary and secondary groups.

7. Explain the most important functions of groups, including the implications of various types of leadership.

8. Discuss the role of reference groups and the phenomenon of anticipatory socialization.

9. Explain how variations in the size of groups affect what goes on within them.

10. Distinguish between the formal and informal structure of associations and explain the importance of the latter.

11. Explain the six defining characteristics of bureaucracy described in Max Weber's ideal type.

12. Explain Robert Michels' concept of "The Iron Law of Oligarchy" and apply it to contemporary society.

13. Explain the importance of social institutions and social organization.

KEY CONCEPTS

Understanding Social Interaction

intimate distance: the social spacing used for intensely personal and private interactions.

personal distance: at about 2.5 to 4 feet, the spacing used by most Americans in ordinary conversation.

social distance: a distance of between 4 and 12 feet, it is used in more impersonal business interactions.

public distance: the type of spacing between an individual and a group in a large formal gathering.

social action: anything people are conscious of doing because of other people.

social interaction: two or more people taking each other into account.

context: the physical setting, social environment, and activities surrounding a social interaction.

norms: specific rules of behavior that are agreed upon and shared and that prescribe limits of acceptable behavior.

Types of Social Interaction

exchange interaction: people doing something for each other with the express purpose of receiving a reward or return.

cooperative interaction: people acting together to promote common interests or achieve shared goals.

spontaneous cooperation: people acting together on the spur of the moment, without any advance planning.

traditional cooperation: cooperative behavior that carries the weight of custom and is passed on from one generation to the next.

directed cooperation: a joint activity that is conducted under the control of people in authority.

contractual cooperation: people agreeing to cooperate in certain specified ways, with each person's obligations clearly spelled out.

conflict: people struggling against one another for some commonly prized object or value.

coercion: a form of conflict in which one of the parties is much stronger than the other and can impose its will on the weaker party.

competition: a form of conflict confined within agreed-upon rules.

Elements of Social Interaction

statuses: socially defined positions that people occupy in a group or society and in terms of which they interact with one another.

master status: one of the multiple statuses a person occupies that seems to dominate the others in patterning a person's life.

ascribed statuses: statuses conferred upon people by virtue of birth or other significant factors not controlled by their own actions or decisions.

achieved statuses: statuses occupied as a result of an individual's actions.

roles: culturally defined rules for proper behavior that are associated with every status.

role set: all the roles attached to a single status.

role strain: conflicting demands attached to the same role.

role conflict: an inability to enact the roles of one status without violating those of another status.

The Nature of Groups

social group: a number of people who have a common identity, some feeling of unity, and certain common goals and shared norms.

social aggregate: people temporarily in physical proximity to one another, but who share little else.

primary group: a group in which members have an emotional investment in one another, know one another intimately, and interact as total individuals rather than through specialized roles.

secondary group: a group that has relatively little intimacy, specific goals, is formally organized, and is impersonal.

Functions of Groups

leader: someone who occupies a central role or position of dominance and influence in a group.

instrumental leadership: a type of leadership in which the leader actively proposes tasks and plans to guide the group toward achieving its goals.

expressive leadership: a type of leadership in which the leader works to keep relations among group members harmonious and group morale high.

reference group: a group or social category that an individual uses to help define beliefs, attitudes, and values and to guide behavior.

Small Groups

small group: a group that actually meets together and has few enough members that all members know one another.

dyad: the smallest possible group, it contains two members.

triad: a group consisting of three members.

subgroup: a splinter group within a larger group.

Large Groups: Associations

association: a purposefully created special-interest group that has clearly defined goals and official ways of doing things.

bureaucracy: a formal, rationally organized social structure with clearly defined patterns of activity in which, ideally, every series of actions is functionally related to the purposes of the organization.

ideal type: an exaggerated model of reality used to illustrate a concept.

oligarchy: the domination of an organization by a small, self-serving, self-perpetuating group of people in positions of power and responsibility.

Institutions and Social Organization

social institutions: the ordered social relationships that grow out of the values, norms, statuses, and roles that organize those activities that fulfill society's fundamental needs.

social organization: the relatively stable pattern of social relationships among individuals and groups in society.

KEY THINKERS/RESEARCHERS

Max Weber: one of the first sociologists to stress the importance of social interaction, he also developed a model of bureaucracy.

Edward T. Hall: a pioneer in studying the context of social interaction.

Charles Horton Cooley: a pioneer in defining and demonstrating the importance of primary groups.

Georg Simmel: the first sociologist to emphasize the effect of the size of a group on the interaction process.

Solomon Asch: conducted important research showing that a substantial proportion of individuals were willing to deny the evidence of their senses to conform to the group.

Robert Michels: a student of bureaucracy, he developed the Iron Law of Oligarchy.

LECTURE SUGGESTIONS

1. **The Context of Social Interaction.** Most professors find that students are often somewhat taken aback when they encounter us in other contexts — at the store, in leisure pursuits, in church, etc. Use your own experience as an example and discuss with students this phenomenon. When we've gotten to know someone in a particular context, it can often be difficult to know how to interact with them in a different context — i.e., different norms and language govern. Ask students for their reactions.

2. **Space as a Context for Social Interaction.** Draw on Edward Hall's work (see Resources) for examples of how different cultures use space differently. You may have people in the class who can speak to this issue based on their personal experiences.

3. **Nonverbal Behavior and Perception of Credibility.** Conduct a relatively harmless experiment several weeks into the course in which you come to class one day *very* sloppily dressed (within your personal tolerance level, of course!). Say nothing to the students, and don't respond to any remarks. Conduct the

class as usual. Near the end, ask students about their reactions to you. Was your credibility affected? How was the interaction altered? Where else does this phenomenon occur?

4. **Verbal and Nonverbal Interaction.** Erving Goffman's work is a rich source of material for examples of interactional behavior. In my experience students have found concepts such as civil inattention (how people politely ignore strangers) and studied nonobservance (how we pretend not to notice obviously embarrassing aspects or behavior of another person) entertaining as well as educational. See especially *The Presentation of Self in Everyday Life*(see Resources), *Interaction Ritual,* and *Stigma.* Some other good sources on nonverbal interaction are cited in the Resources section below.

5. **Gender and Nonverbal Interaction.** As Tischler states, many gender differences have been noted in the norms for interaction. A source which can provide many good examples for illustration of this point in class is Nancy Henley's *Body Politics* (see Resources).

6. **Social Aggregate vs. Social Group.** It can be an interesting exercise to pose a number of situations to the class and have them decide whether the actors constitute an aggregate or a group (examples may be found in the Study Guide). Working through a number of different examples forces students to think clearly about those qualities of social interaction that distinguish a group.

7. **Primary vs. Secondary Groups.** Table 5-1 lists a variety of characteristics of primary and secondary groups. Students are often intimidated at the prospect of trying to memorize this long list. Of course they don't have to. The important thing is to understand the key distinguishing features, and then reason everything else out from there. For me, the key thing that distinguishes primary from secondary groups is *intimacy* — primary groups have it, secondary groups don't. Lead the class through a reasoning process around the issue of intimacy — what are the preconditions for its existence (small size, durability, intrinsic valuation, etc.) and what are the results of its existence (inclusive knowledge, informality, spontaneity, etc.)? If students can reason this through, then they really understand the concept.

8. **Weber's Model of Bureaucracy.** In the Resources section is a handout summarizing Weber's model. It parallels pretty closely the material in the text, but adds some additional information as well. I have found that giving students a handout like this (1) emphasizes its importance, and (2) provides them with a handy tool they can use in other contexts. After passing out the handout, you may want to model the process by analyzing a sample bureaucracy according to the criteria. See if students can do the same.

9. **Functions of Bureaucracy.** Bureaucracy may not be a dirty word to everyone; it may actually serve some useful and valuable functions. Discuss these with the class, and see if you can elicit from them situations in which bureaucracy is desirable (e.g., law and the courts). On the other hand, bureaucracy is legendary for its dysfunctions. I summarize some of the main problems in another potential handout in the Resources section at the end of this chapter.

10. **Institutions and Habits.** One way of getting students to understand institutions is to encourage them to see institutions on the collective level as equivalent to habits on the individual level. Both involve standardizing patterns in order to save time and energy. Both are made necessary by the lack of instinctual determinism in humans. You may want to begin with habits, pointing out some common ones (Why do students always sit in the same seats, even when seats are not assigned? Why does each individual have a ritualized, not spontaneous, way of getting dressed in the morning and attending to personal hygiene? etc.) and asking students why they have developed habits, and what purpose these habits serve. Then generalize this to institutions on the collective level.

SUGGESTED ACTIVITIES

1. **Norms and Social Interaction.** Ethnomethodologists tell us that we can best understand the significance of social rules by systematically violating them. Assign students, after appropriate ethical briefing, to violate some common norms (see, e.g., examples in text) and then share their experiences with the class. Try to draw out gender, ethnicity, age, and/or social class differences.

2. **Gender and Nonverbal Interaction.** Divide the class into small groups that are homogeneous by sex. Have the groups talk about cues they employ to get the attention of members of the opposite sex and to flirt with them. Pair the groups up or in the class as a whole discuss gender differences in these cues and possible misinterpretations.

3. **Types of Social Interaction.** Have students keep a journal for a week in which they record the types of interactions in which they engage throughout the day. Then have them classify and count these interactions. Does one type predominate? What can they learn about their lives from this? Given the type of interaction that predominates, do students feel that they have adequate skills to engage in it? Why or why not?

4. **Competition vs. Cooperation.** In class play the Prisoner's Dilemma game (described in a wide variety of handbooks) to give students a feel for the choices involved in competition and cooperation.

5. **Status.** If students haven't previously done the Who Am I? exercise (Chapter 1 of this manual or Chapter 4 of the Study Guide), have them do it now. When they are finished, have them code the statuses listed as ascribed or achieved, and have them identify their master status. Have a discussion of the relative importance of ascription and achievement in their lives.

6. **Role Strain and Role Conflict.** An easy and popular learning exercise is to have students write about and/or discuss role strain and role conflict in their lives. Work toward deriving some generalizations about roles, role conflict and role strain in modern society.

7. **Role Playing.** As per Berger's quote in the text, self-perception can be profoundly affected by the roles we play. Do some role-playing exercises in class. Especially good are those that involve role reversals or other situations in which students may be moved to an empathic understanding of another's attitudes, feelings, and behavior. One suggestion would be to have a male worker complain to his unsympathetic/unbelieving female boss about his being sexually harassed. Or it could be a male citizen filing a formal complaint with a female (or a male) police sergeant. Many role-playing exercises are described in material available from the ASA Teaching Resources Center (see Introduction). One caution: students should never be compelled to engage in any exercise with which they are uncomfortable. Stress to them that they always have the right to say no before and anytime during an exercise.

8. **Characteristics of Groups.** Have students engage in an exercise similar to that in the Study Guide in which they discuss in small groups how the group carries out its six major tasks. If you want to be a little cute, you can make their task for analysis the process of carrying out the very task you have assigned them.

9. **Reference Groups.** Have students make lists of their major reference groups, then discuss similarities and differences, not only in who these groups are, but also in their level of abstraction and/or distance from the individual.

10. Informal Structure of Associations. Have students engage in an exercise similar to that in the Study Guide in which they describe the informal structure of an association, knowledge of which allows successful interaction with and within that association.

RESOURCES FOR INSTRUCTORS

Roger E. Axtell, Gestures: *The Do's and Taboos of Body Language Around the World.* New York: Wiley, 1991.

Erving Goffman, *Interaction Ritual.* Chicago: Aldine, 1967.

Nancy Henley, *Body Politics: Power, Sex, and Nonverbal Communication.* Englewood Cliffs, NJ: Prentice Hall 1977.

Peter Marsh (ed.), *Eye to Eye: How People Interact.* Topsfield, MA: Salem House Publishers, 1988.

RESOURCES FOR STUDENTS

Understanding Social Interaction

Peter L. Berger and Thomas Luckmann, *The Social Construction of Reality.* Garden City, NY: Anchor Books, 1967.
> A classic treatise that argues that social reality only exists to the extent and in the fashion that it is created through social interaction.

William H.Whyte, *City: Rediscovering the Center.* New York: Doubleday, 1988.
> Fascinating study of how the physical layout of space in downtown areas structures social interaction.

Types of Social Interaction

Edward T. Hall, *The Hidden Dimension.* New York: Doubleday, 1966.
> A survey of the way different cultures use space and how this affects their patterns of interaction and communication.

Elements of Social Interaction

Erving Goffman, *The Presentation of Self in Everyday Life.* Garden City, NY: Doubleday, 1959.
> Goffman lays out, in a highly readable and entertaining fashion, his dramaturgical view of social interaction.

Bureaucracy

Rosabeth Moss Kanter and Barry A. Stein, eds., *Life in Organizations: Workplaces as People Experience Them.* New York: Basic Books, 1979.
> Slices of life from all levels and phases of contemporary bureaucracy.

MAX WEBER'S "IDEAL TYPE" BUREAUCRACY

DEFINITION: A complex, hierarchical authority structure that operates under explicit rules and procedures.

CHARACTERISTICS:

1.   **Clear-Cut Division of Labor**

   Each office or bureau has a specialized sphere of competence.

   Job descriptions are explicit.

2.   **Hierarchy of Authority**

   Organization is shaped like a pyramid (or, more exactly, like the Eiffel Tower —
        i.e., small, narrow top and flat, wide bottom.)

   The scope of authority of each office and each level is clearly defined;

   The organizational chart indicates reporting lines.

3.   **Elaborate System of Rules**

   Everyday actions are governed by explicit procedures which are a rational application of the governing principles or mission.

4.   **Impersonal Detachment**

   All customers/clients are treated as impersonal "cases".

   Universalistic, not particularistic, criteria are applied.

5.   **Extensive Written Records are Kept**

   Records of both procedures and cases are recorded.

   "The Files" become the basis for rational evaluation and planning.

6.   **Office-Holding as a Professional Vocation**

   The office is *not* the personal property of the individual.

   The commitment of the individual officeholder is to the *office*, not to other individuals.

   Hiring is done on the basis of technical standards and credentials.

   Promotion is on the basis of seniority and/or merit.

   The individual has the opportunity to build a career.

   Career = a sequence of work experiences that build on one another in terms of
   increasing skill, experience, responsibility and rewards.

73

DYSFUNCTIONS OF BUREAUCRACY

1) EXCESSIVE RATIONALITY

Subordination of humans and human ends to impersonal, technical goals.

2) INEFFICIENCY IN THE FACE OF NOVEL CIRCUMSTANCES

Inability to cope with situations outside of "Standard Operating Procedure." Thorstein Veblen called this "Trained Incapacity."

3) ORGANIZATIONAL INERTIA

Its own continued existence becomes the organization's *raison d'etre*.

4) COMMUNICATION DISTORTION

Narrow job descriptions and roles provide a limited basis for common communication. Distortions are inevitable, especially at the middle and lower levels.

5) CREATION OF SELF-DEFEATING PERSONALITIES AND COPING MECHANISMS

Authoritarian structure limits the creativity and personal development of individuals and results in coping mechanisms that undermine the efficiency of the organization.

Coping Mechanisms: (1) Compulsive Rebelliousness

                       (2) Identification With Authority

                       (3) Resignation

CHAPTER SIX: Deviant Behavior and Social Control

CHAPTER OUTLINE

Defining Normal and Deviant Behavior
> Making Moral Judgments
> The Functions of Deviance
> The Dysfunctions of Deviance

Mechanisms of Social Control
> Internal Means of Control
> External Means of Control: Sanctions
>> Positive and Negative Sanctions
>> Formal and Informal Sanctions
>> A Typology of Sanctions

Theories of Crime and Deviance
> Biological Theories of Deviance
> Psychological Theories of Deviance
>> Psychoanalytic Theory
>> Behavioral Theories
>> Crime as Individual Choice
> *Taking the Sociological Perspective: Domestic Violence Against Women: A Historical Perspective*
> Sociological Theories of Deviance
>> Anomie Theory
>> Strain Theory
>> Control Theory
>> Techniques of Neutralization
>> Cultural Transmission Theory
>> Labeling Theory

The Importance of Law
> The Emergence of Laws

Crime in the United States
> Crime Statistics
> *Sociology at Work: Interview with Jack Levin: Serial Murderers and Mass Murderers*

Kinds of Crime in the United States
> Juvenile Crime
> Violent Crime
> Property Crime
> White-Collar Crime
> Victimless Crime
> Victims of Crime

Criminal Justice in the United States
> The Police
> The Courts
> Prisons
>>   Goals of Imprisonment
> A Shortage of Prisons
> Women in Prison
> The Funnel Effect
> *Controversies in Sociology: The Continuing Debate over Capital Punishment: Does it Deter Murderers?*

LEARNING OBJECTIVES

1. Understand deviance as culturally relative.

2. Explain the functions and dysfunctions of deviance.

3. Distinguish between internal and external means of social control.

4. Differentiate among the various types of sanctions.

5. Describe and critique biological and psychological theories of deviance.

6. Discuss the concept of anomie and its role in producing deviance.

7. Explain how the strain between cultural goals and lack of means to attain them can lead to crime.

8. Explain the basic assumptions of control theory.

9. Explain and give examples of techniques of neutralization.

10. Explain how deviance is culturally transmitted.

11. Explain the process of labeling and the distinction between primary and secondary deviance.

12. Contrast consensus and conflict perspectives on the origin of a society's legal code.

13. Compare the *Uniform Crime Reports* and the *National Crime Victimization Survey* as sources of information about the crime rate.

14. Distinguish among the major types of crime.

15. Describe how crime rates vary among socioeconomic groups.

16. Describe the major features of the criminal justice system in the United States.

17. Describe and assess important current issues with regard to prisons.

18. Describe the funnel effect and discuss its implications.

KEY CONCEPTS

Defining Normal and Deviant Behavior

moral code: the symbolic system in terms of which behavior takes on the quality of being good or bad, right or wrong.

normal behavior: behavior that conforms to the rules or norms of the group in which it occurs.

deviant behavior: behavior that fails to conform to the rules or norms of a group in which it occurs.

Mechanisms of Social Control

mechanisms of social control: ways of directing or influencing members to conform to the group's values and norms.

internal means of control: the operation of a group's moral code on an individual even in the absence of reactions by others.

external means of control: the responses of other people to an individual's behavior.

sanctions: rewards and penalties by a group's members that are used to regulate an individual's behavior.

positive sanctions: actions that encourage an individual to continue acting in a certain way (i.e., rewards).

negative sanctions: actions that discourage the repetition or continuation of a behavior (i.e., punishments).

formal sanctions: sanctions applied in a public ritual, usually under the direct or indirect control of authorities.

informal sanctions: sanctions applied spontaneously by group members with little or no formal direction.

informal positive sanctions: displays people use spontaneously to express their approval of another's behavior.

informal negative sanctions: spontaneous displays of disapproval or displeasure.

formal positive sanctions: public affairs, rituals, or ceremonies that express social approval of a person's behavior.

formal negative sanctions: actions that express institutionalized disapproval of a person's behavior.

Theories of Crime and Deviance

anomie: a state of normlessness, in which values and norms have little impact and the culture no longer provides adequate guidelines for behavior.

innovators: individuals who accept the culturally validated goal of success but find deviant ways of achieving it.

ritualists: individuals who reject or deemphasize the importance of success and instead concentrate on following and enforcing rules more precisely than was ever intended.

retreatists: people who pull back from society altogether and cease to pursue culturally legitimate goals.

rebels: people who reject both the goals and the institutionalized means to achieve them, and wish to build a different social order with alternative goals and means.

techniques of neutralization: a thought process that makes it possible to justify illegal or deviant behavior.

theory of differential association: the idea that individuals learn criminal techniques and attitudes through with intimate contact with deviants.

labeling theory: the theory that focuses on the social process by which a person comes to be defined as deviant and the consequences of that definition for the individual.

primary deviance: the original behavior that leads to the application of a label to an individual.

secondary deviance: behavior that people develop as a result of having been labeled as deviant.

The Importance of Law

legal code: the body of formal rules adopted by a society's political authority.

laws: formal rules.

consensus approach: assumes that laws are merely a formal expression of the agreed-upon norms and values of the people.

conflict approach: argues that the elite use their power to enact and enforce laws that support their own economic interests, to the exclusion of the interests of others.

Crime in the United States

crime: any behavior that violates a society's criminal laws.

violent crime: an unlawful event that may result in injury to a person.

property crime: an unlawful act committed with the intent of gaining property, but that does not involve the use or threat of force against an individual.

felonies: the most serious crimes, usually punishable by a year or more in prison.

misdemeanors: less serious violations of criminal law or minor offenses.

Kinds of Crime in the United States

juvenile crime: the breaking of criminal laws by individuals younger than eighteen.

recidivism: repeated criminal behavior after punishment.

status offense: behavior that is criminal only because the person involved is a minor.

diversion: steering offenders away from the justice system to social agencies.

white-collar crime: acts by individuals who, while occupying positions of social responsibility or high prestige, break the the law in the course of their work.

victimless crimes: acts that violate those laws meant to enforce the moral code.

Criminal Justice in the United States

criminal justice system: personnel and procedures for arrest, trial, and punishment.

rehabilitation: the resocialization of criminals to conform to society's values and norms and the teaching of usable work habits and skills.

funnel effect: the fact that, of the many crimes committed, few seem to result in punishment of the offender.

KEY THINKERS/RESEARCHERS

Émile Durkheim: argued that deviant behavior is an integral part of all healthy societies; developed the concept of anomie.

Cesare Lombroso: suggested that criminals were evolutionary throwbacks who could be identified by primitive physical features, particularly with regard to the head.

William H. Sheldon: identified three main body types and suggested that each was responsible for different personality traits.

Sigmund Freud: argued that crime is produced by the unconscious impulses of the individual.

James Q. Wilson and Richard Herrnstein: argue that crime is the product of a rational choice by an individual as a result of weighing the costs and benefits of alternative courses of action.

Robert K. Merton: developed a theory of structural strain to explain deviance.

Travis Hirschi: developed control theory, in which it is hypothesized that the strength of social bonds keep most of us from becoming criminals.

Gresham Sykes and David Matza: argued that deviants learn techniques of neutralization to justify their deviance.

Clifford Shaw and Henry McKay: suggested that certain neighborhoods generate a culture of crime that is passed on to residents.

Edwin H. Sutherland: developed the theory of differential association to explain why some people and not others become deviant; coined the term *white-collar crime.*

Edwin Lemert: pioneered the development of labeling theory.

LECTURE SUGGESTIONS

1. **Deviant vs. Normal Behavior.** Many students are not used to thinking of deviance as relative. Using Chapter 3 of the text and the resources in this Instructor's Manual as a guide, present students with cultural practices that are normal in one culture but deviant in others. Or deviant within the larger culture, but normal within a subculture. In Chapter 5 students learned about the importance of context in shaping the meaning of social interaction. It would be useful to remind them of that fact here. Individualistically-oriented American students also need to be reminded that deviance is *socially* defined, and it is not just a matter of individuals deciding for themselves what they will or won't accept as normal behavior. The norms are collectively established and enforced. Give students examples of behaviors that have changed categories, from normal to deviant, or from deviant to normal (e.g., smoking cigarettes, men wearing cologne or earrings). Prompt students to come up with more examples.

2. **"Doing the Right Thing" vs. Doing the Wrong Thing.** Many good illustrations of the issue of the relativity of deviance can be found in Spike Lee's film *Do The Right Thing* (fairly widely available for rental). The title itself implies a moral injunction. In the film, definitions of deviance vary by age, gender, ethnicity, race, occupation, and social class. Moreover, some definitions are altered in the course of the film. I think that this film's sociological sophistication and richness in themes that can be used in class can justify using class time to show the entire film (about 2 hours). Alternatively, you could arrange for or require students to view the film outside of class. One caution: Much of the language is ghetto street language, and it is pretty raw for some students. They may be offended by constant use of the f-word. You will have to be sensitive to this, and make a decision based on local standards. I don't think the portrayal of street life and the use of raw language is egregious or deliberately offensive. I think Spike Lee has accurately and faithfully depicted one aspect of central city subculture, and therefore it is legitimate and valuable. But you must decide for yourself.

3. **Making Moral Judgments.** Tischler observes that some acts seem to be almost universally accepted as deviant, and that sociologists are willing to classify some human actions as absolutely deviant. Tischler doesn't, however, discuss by what standards this is decided. I would suggest that one standard that is used is that of basic human needs (see discussion in Chapter 3 of this manual). Using this criterion allows us to say that some actions are deviant because they are anti-human — i.e., they prevent or inhibit human growth and development.

4. **The Functions of Deviance.** Again, many students are not used to thinking of deviance as having positive functions for the social order. This is a point worth emphasizing, and there is a great deal of sociological literature from which to draw in illustrating this point. You may want to provide additional examples of each function of deviance, then ask the class to provide more.

5. **The Functions of Tabloid Journalism.** As a way of getting at the functions of deviance, bring in selected tabloid newspaper headlines, descriptions of TV talk show topics, or perhaps videotapes of the promotional commercials announcing the juicy topic of the day on a particular talk show. Ask students to speculate about the role of these newspapers and TV shows in fulfilling the functions of deviance.

6. **Another Function of Deviance.** A function of deviance not explicitly mentioned by Tischler, but referenced indirectly by his discussion of Thoreau at the beginning of the chapter, is the role of deviance in promoting social change. Tell students about the early civil rights, anti-war, feminist, environmental, etc. movements, and how the activists were painted as troublesome malcontents. Over time, however, the deviants of each movement wound up promoting social change that was functional for maintaining society.

7. **Another Dysfunction of Deviance.** When deviance goes unpunished, it not only disrupts the social order, but it undermines internal social control — the "will to conform." This dysfunction seems particularly salient in contemporary society. Ask students how often they have felt "Why should I be a sucker or a chump and do the right thing when no one else seems to?" About what issues have they felt this way?

8. **Internal vs. External Means of Control.** Discuss the fact that, in contemporary American society, community as the basis for reinforcing internal social control has been severely undermined. The result of this is a greater reliance on external means of control. A good example is the increasingly elaborate electronic and video surveillance found in stores because customers (and employees) can no longer be trusted not to shoplift or steal because it would be wrong. Ask students to speculate about why this has happened and what the implications are for society and individuals of increasing reliance on external means of control.

9. **Theories of Crime and Deviance.** Invite into class, as a panel or as individual guest lecturers, persons involved with the criminal justice system: e.g., police officer, judge, prosecuting attorney, public defender, probation officer, etc. Ask your students to decode the presentations in terms of the underlying theory of deviance being employed. Students can do this as a writing assignment and/or a discussion in a subsequent class.

10. **The Importance of Law.** Sir Thomas More, former Lord Chancellor of England, was executed under orders from King Henry VIII because More would not accede to the law as Henry wished it to be. More argued that he followed a higher law. Nonetheless, More did not reject the rule of law in civil society. There several wonderful scenes in the award-winning movie about the More/Henry struggle, *A Man for All Seasons,* where Sir Thomas lectures family members or peers about the importance of the rule of law. These short excerpts would be useful discussion-starters in class. The movie is widely rentable, or you could get the screenplay (by Robert Bolt) and have students volunteer to read the parts in class.

11. **Crime Statistics.** It is useful to discuss with students the problems with crime statistics so that they don't simply take the statistics at face value. It is helpful to have examples as well — for instance, the mysterious improvement in crime rate figures just prior to a local election.

12. **Juvenile Crime.** Invite a juvenile probation officer and/or juvenile offenders into class to discuss the background motivation and social milieu for their offenses. For many students, this would be a real eye-opener.

13. **White-Collar Crime vs. Street Crime.** To illustrate Tischler's point that the economic impact of white-collar crimes is far greater than that of street crimes, bring in current examples, such as the S&L crisis, BCCI, federal contractor fraud, price fixing, securities fraud, etc. — there seem to be no shortage of examples. This could also be an assignment for students — search the media for reports of white-collar crime. It is also instructive for you or the students to note the punishments meted out to those found guilty of white-collar vs. street crimes.

14. **White-Collar Crime.** The text barely skims the surface of this topic. You may want to talk to the class about corporate, governmental, and organizational crime. A good source on corporate crime is *Mother Jones* magazine, which has won numerous awards for its investigative reports on this subject. An issue that combines crime by professional workers with organizational deviance in covering it up is sexual abuse by the clergy. A good source here is Shupe's *In the Name of All That's Holy: A Theory of Clergy Malfeasance* (see Resources).

15. **The U.S. Criminal Justice System.** Since many students will not have had much contact with most of the criminal justice system, it is important to make them aware of how it actually works. There are a number of very good films on policing and prisons. You may also want to consider inviting guest speakers or a panel of people involved with the criminal justice system. In many locations, there are people who are, formally or informally, "professional court watchers." If you can identify such a person or persons, invite them in to talk with the class about what they observe.

SUGGESTED ACTIVITIES

1. **Typology of Sanctions.** As an exercise, hand out a blank 2x2 table similar to Figure 6-1 in the text. Ask students, working in small groups, to generate examples of each of the four types of sanctions relative to a particular environment — e.g., college.

2. **Analyzing Theories of Crime and Deviance.** Duplicate the blank chart in the Resources section at the end of this chapter and distribute it to students. Working in small groups, ask students to fill in the chart. In order to save time, you may want to assign different portions of the chart to different groups. Each group should have several theories to work with, however, so that they can see the contrast. Have students present their work to the class as a whole. You may want to make a transparency of a blank chart and fill it in with the main points raised during the discussion. That way you can make sure that students get the main points as well as the benefit of class discussion.

3. **Merton's Typology of Modes of Adaptation.** A good discussion can almost always be generated around asking students to come up with examples of each mode of adaptation. Narrow the discussion down to an environment with which students are familiar — e.g., school or work. Ask students to think about the implications of having a majority of society in each of the categories. What things would be better, and what things would be worse?

4. **Criminal Activity Flow Chart.** Assign students, working in small groups (during or outside of class), to construct a flow chart illustrating the stages in the life history of a crime and criminal. Begin with the inputs into the commission of a crime, and then move through each stage of the legal and criminal justice system, illustrating the many branching possibilities at each stage.

5. **Victimless Crimes.** Ask students to discuss, in small groups, whether or not they think these crimes are truly "victimless." Are there other crimes they would remove from or add to the list? Why?

6. **Courts and Prisons.** If time and your situation permit, take the class on a field trip to the courthouse or a jail/prison. What most students know about these environments is only what they have seen on TV; experiencing the situation in the first person is often a major eye-opener for them. It may seem that a field trip takes too much time away from class activities, but, handled properly, a field trip for which students are properly prepared and debriefed can provide an unforgettable educational experience.

RESOURCES FOR INSTRUCTORS

Anson Shupe, *In the Name of All That's Holy: A Theory of Clergy Malfeasance.* Westport, CN: Praeger, 1995.

RESOURCES FOR STUDENTS

Defining Normal and Deviant Behavior

Kai Erikson, *Wayward Puritans: A Study in the Sociology of Deviance.* New York, John Wiley, 1966.
> A classic work in which the author shows how the early Puritan settlers in America used deviance to maintain group solidarity.

Theories of Crime and Deviance

Delos H. Kelly, *Deviant Behavior: A Text-Reader in the Sociology of Deviance, Third Edition.* New York: St. Martin's, 1989.
> A comprehensive look at theories and types of deviance. Includes many of the classic and/or definitive writings in each area.

Kinds of Crime in the United States

Russell Mokhiber, *Corporate Crime and Violence: Big Business Power and the Abuse of the Public Trust.* San Francisco: Sierra Club Books, 1988.
> A catalog of crimes by multinational corporations that resulted in serious injury and death. This is an area that is often overlooked, even in discussions of white-collar crime.

Criminal Justice in the United States

John Irwin, *The Felon.* Englewood Cliffs, NJ: Prentice Hall, 1970.
> Based on two years of participant observation and in-depth interviews with felons, this study follows career criminals from their beginnings in crime through the prison and post-prison experience.

Jeffrey Reiman, *The Rich Get Richer and the Poor Get Prison: Ideology, Class, and Criminal Justice, Third Edition.* New York: Macmillan, 1990.
> A critical look at the entire American criminal justice system.

ANALYZING THEORIES OF CRIME AND DEVIANCE

Theory	Basic Assumption	Cause of Deviance	Implications for Social Policy
Biological			
Psycho-analysis			
Behaviorism			
Individual Choice			
Anomie			
Strain Theory			
Control Theory			
Techniques of Neutralization			
Cultural Transmission			
Labeling Theory			

84

CHAPTER SEVEN: Social Stratification

CHAPTER OUTLINE

The Nature of Social Stratification
> Social Mobility
>> Factors Affecting Social Mobility

Stratification Systems
> The Caste System
> The Estate System
> The Class System
> *Sociology at Work: How the Other Half Lives: Life in Distressed Neighborhoods*

The Dimensions of Social Stratification
> Economics
> Power
> Prestige
> Occupational Stratification

Theories of Stratification
> The Functionalist Theory
>> The Immorality of Social Stratification
>> The Neglect of Talent and Merit
>> Barriers to Free Competition
>> Functionally Important Jobs
> Conflict Theory
>> Karl Marx
>> Max Weber
> Modern Conflict Theory
> The Need for Synthesis
> *Controversies in Sociology: What Causes the Gap Between the Rich and the Poor?*

LEARNING OBJECTIVES

1. Explain the relationship of social evaluation to social inequality and social stratification.

2. Explain the different conditions and types of social mobility.

3. Explain the factors that affect one's chances of upward social mobility.

4. Compare and contrast the caste, estate, and class systems.

5. Define wealth and describe its distribution in the United States by race and ethnicity.

6. Contrast differing views of power in American society.

7. Describe the pattern of occupational stratification by prestige in U.S. society.

8. Summarize and critique the functionalist theory of stratification.

9. Explain the main points of Karl Marx's conflict theory.

10. Explain Max Weber's multidimensional view of stratification.

11. Describe the key features of modern conflict theory.

KEY CONCEPTS

The Nature of Social Stratification

social inequality: the uneven distribution of privileges, material rewards, opportunities, power, prestige, and influence among individuals or groups.

social stratification: the division of society into levels, steps, or positions that is perpetuated by the society's major institutions.

social mobility: movement of an individual or a group from one social status to another.

open society: characterized by the attempt to provide equal opportunity for everyone to compete for desired statuses.

closed society: a society in which the various aspects of people's lives are determined at birth and remain fixed.

horizontal mobility: a change in status with no corresponding change in social class.

vertical mobility: a change in status that results in a change in social class.

intergenerational mobility: a change in social status that takes place over two or more generations.

intragenerational mobility: a change in social status that occurs within the lifetime of one individual.

status inconsistency: situations in which people rank differently on certain stratification characteristics than on others.

Stratification Systems

caste system: a rigid form of stratification based on ascribed characteristics such as skin color or family identity.

estate system: a closed system of stratification in which a person's social position is defined by law and membership is determined primarily by inheritance.

estate: a segment of a society that has legally established rights and duties.

social class: a category of people who share similar opportunities, economic and vocational positions, lifestyles, attitudes, and behavior.

class system: a society that contains several different social classes and permits at least some social mobility.

The Dimensions of Social Stratification

wealth: the total economic assets of an individual or family.

power: the ability of an individual or group to attain goals, control events, and maintain influence over others, even in the face of opposition.

power elite: the group of people who control policy making and the setting of priorities.

prestige: the approval and respect an individual or group receives from other members of society.

Theories of Stratification

bourgeoisie: the owners of the means of production or capital.

proletariat: the working class.

KEY THINKERS/RESEARCHERS

C. Wright Mills: proposed the concept of a power elite governing American society.

G. William Domhoff: suggested that America is controlled by a governing class whose members are very rich, intermarry, attend the same schools, and spend their time in the same clubs.

Arnold Rose: argued that American society is characterized by multiple power structures that, even though dominated by elites, tend to balance each other out.

Kingsley Davis and Wilbert Moore: developed the functionalist theory of stratification.

Karl Marx: a pioneering conflict theorist, he developed a critique of capitalist class society and a vision of the transition to socialism.

Max Weber: proposed that stratification takes place on the basis of class, status, and power.

Ralf Dahrendorf: suggested that functionalist and conflict theories of stratification are really complementary rather than opposed.

LECTURE SUGGESTIONS

1. **Relative Equality in Hunting and Gathering Societies.** The idea of humans living together in a situation of roughly equal access to resources is unfathomable to many students — so unfathomable that they have a hard time believing that it ever happened, much less that humans lived this way for the majority of time our species has been on this planet. It is therefore useful to show them some real-life examples. A wide variety of films in anthropology portray social life in hunting and gathering societies.

Also, readily accessible is the video *The Gods Must Be Crazy*. The first fifteen minutes or so of this film are essentially a documentary look at life among the !Kung San in the Kalahari Desert of southwestern Africa (particularly relevant in that Tischler mentions them in this chapter). Actually, you may want to let the film run longer, because the plot involves a coke bottle that mysteriously drops from the sky (from a passing airplane). Its unexpected presence threatens to disrupt the culture — in part by creating inequality — and therefore it must be gotten rid of. The rest of the film portrays the experiences of the protagonist in trying to return the bottle.

2. **Vertical Social Mobility in the United States.** Pose these questions to the class: Has America historically been a land of opportunity — i.e., a place where upward social mobility is possible? Is it a land of opportunity today? The answer to the question must take into account the distinction between intergenerational and intragenerational mobility. Make sure that students are aware of the difference. Also, note to the class (as Tischler does) that *downward* mobility is also a possibility.

3. **Gender and Social Mobility.** Point out to the class that nearly all of the research to date on social mobility has been done with *male* subjects. Ask the class to suggest why this may be so. Also ask them how they think this bias might distort the data. Finally, ask them to speculate on what we are likely to find when we include women equally in the research.

4. **Resistance and Change in a Caste System.** Tischler notes in this chapter that "Hindus have never placidly accepted the caste system." Another caste system, closer to home, that was never fully accepted is the slave system of the antebellum American South. You may want to illustrate Tischler's point with examples of slave resistance. A good source is Genovese's *Roll, Jordan, Roll: The World the Slaves Made* (see Resources section at the end of this chapter).

5. **Everyday Life in an Estate System.** Except for romantic depictions of castle life, students probably know even less about the estate system of medieval Europe than they do about the caste system of India. A good source of material for giving students a sense of what it was like to live in an estate system is the volume of *A History of Private Life* dealing with the medieval world (see Resources section). For information on the experience of women in this system I would suggest Anderson and Zinsser, *A History of Their Own: Women in Europe from Prehistory to the Present* (see Resources).

6. **Opportunity and Social Mobility.** Most college students agree with the core of the equal opportunity ideology — i.e., each individual should be judged on the basis of his or her own achievements, and not on the basis of inherited characteristics over which they have no control: sex, ethnicity/race, family background, etc. After all, the majority of these students expect to obtain at least some economic payoff from the education they are acquiring. Moreover, they have learned earlier in the chapter that, in American society, education seems to be the single most important factor in upward social mobility. However, most students also support the practice of family inheritance. Point out this contradiction to them by first asking them if they agree with the principles of equal opportunity. Most will. Then suggest to them that, given this view, they probably all support a 100 percent inheritance tax, right? After all, why should some individuals benefit because they happen to be born into a wealthy family? And why should others be punished by having poor parents? In neither case did individual choice or merit have anything to do with it. So, to be consistent, they support confiscatory inheritance taxes, right? NOT!!! This deliberate (but ethical and pedagogically sound) provocation never fails to generate a lively class discussion.

7. **Marx's Theory of Inequality.** Most students are not likely to be familiar with the ideas of Marx, and therefore have to struggle with them a bit more. Two easily-accessible, short explanations of Marx's ideas are Jalee, *How Capitalism Works* and Rius, *Marx for Beginners* (see Resources).

SUGGESTED ACTIVITIES

1. **Social Differentiation vs. Social Evaluation.** Working in small groups, have students generate lists of social differences among people. What differences are implicated in social inequality? Is this justified? Why or why not? See if students can develop principles by which inequality, or certain kinds of inequality, can be justified? Encourage students with different points of view to express themselves. Is it possible to have recognition — even celebration — of differences without differentially evaluating them? Have the students identify under what conditions this can happen.

2. **Status Inconsistency.** Ask students to brainstorm a list of people, positions, or occupations in society that exhibit status inconsistency. On what dimensions of stratification are they inconsistent? Is there a recognizable pattern? What are the implications of these inconsistencies? Are they very problematic? How important is it to have statuses be congruent?

3. **Expectations for Upward Social Mobility.** In small groups, have students discuss their own personal expectations for upward social mobility. Have them share information about the source of their aspirations, the strength and realism of their expectations, and possible barriers to their realization.

4. **Evaluating Occupational Prestige.** Prior to beginning this section of the course, pass out a list of occupations culled from Table 7-1. Ask the students to rate the prestige of each occupation on a 100-point scale. When you reach the discussion of stratification, return student's rankings to them, including some measures of central tendency for the class as a whole. Discuss how closely the students' rankings approximate the national data in Table 7-1, and reasons for both consistencies and inconsistencies.

5. **Inequality and Theories of Stratification.** I use the following exercise to test the accuracy of students' perceptions of inequality and to elicit their assumptions about the necessity of stratification. Your first task is to do some research and ascertain the median annual incomes of 6–10 occupations (see Census Bureau publications or the *Monthly Labor Review*). The more specific the occupational designations are, the better. Make sure that you choose a range of occupations (blue-, white- and pink-collar, industrial and service, etc.) and that you have both traditionally male as well as traditionally female occupations. Next create a chart or overhead transparency that lists the individual occupations and the *grand total* of all their median incomes *only*. In class, divide students into small groups and then show them the list of occupations and the income total. Tell students that their task is to distribute the income total (and *only* that amount) among the listed occupations on the basis of 1) how they perceive it actually was distributed in the year in question; and 2) how they think it *should* have been. Tell students to expect some disagreement in their groups; tell them you will accept minority reports. When students have completed their task (or you have run out of allotted class time), ask each group for its answer(s) and its rationale(s). I have done this exercise many times, and a clear pattern is that most students seem to overestimate how highly-paid the high-prestige occupations are and to underestimate how poorly-compensated the lower occupations are. I emphasize to students that they apparently do not have an accurate picture of inequality in their heads presently, yet they would analyze and act on the social world more effectively if they did. With regard to the second task, when students are permitted to alter the distribution of income, most of them play "Robin Hood" — i.e., take from the rich and give to the poor. I point out that this is actually the strategy followed by political liberals, and one that informs such ideas as the graduated income tax. At this point I usually try to be a little provocative and ask (if a student hasn't done so already) why, in order to simplify the exercise, students didn't simply divide the total income by n and give everyone the average. In response, students lay out the functionalist theory of stratification — talent, risk, responsibility, education, motivation, etc. It's uncanny, but I've found I don't need to lecture on the functionalist theory — students either already know it or this discussion brings it out. While writing students' reasons for the necessity of inequality on the board, I use the opportunity to bring in the

critique of the functionalist theory discussed in Tischler, as well as the conflict theory interpretation. Coming at it this way, I've found, really gets students to think about their assumptions. You may want to have them write a paper reflecting upon the arguments afterward.

RESOURCES FOR INSTRUCTORS

Bonnie S. Anderson and Judith P. Zinsser, *A History of Their Own: Women in Europe from Prehistory to the Present, Vol. I.* New York: Harper & Row, 1988.

Georges Duby (ed.), *A History of Private Life, Vol. II: Revelations of the Medieval World.* trans. by Arthur Goldhammer. Cambridge, MA: Belknap/Harvard University Press, 1988.

Eugene D. Genovese, *Roll, Jordan, Roll: The World the Slaves Made.* New York: Pantheon, 1974.

Pierre Jalée, *How Capitalism Works.* New York: Monthly Review Press, 1977.

Rius, *Marx for Beginners.* New York: Pantheon.

RESOURCES FOR STUDENTS

The Nature of Social Stratification
Barbara Ehrenreich, *Fear of Falling: The Inner Life of the Middle Class.* New York: Pantheon, 1989.
   A perceptive analysis of how the economic pressures that have forced many out of the middle class play themselves out in political attitudes and behavior.

D. Stanley Eitzen and Maxine Baca Zinn, eds., *The Reshaping of America.* Englewood Cliffs, NJ: Prentice Hall, 1989.
   A collection of articles examining the forces transforming contemporary American society and the impact of these changes on people's life chances.

Stratification Systems
Oliver C. Cox, *Caste, Class, and Race: A Study in Social Dynamics.* New York: Monthly Review Press, 1970.
   A comprehensive, landmark analysis of the concepts of caste and class (including estates) and their relevance/application to the issues of race in American society.

The Dimensions of Social Stratification
G. William Domhoff, *Who Rules America Now: A View for the 80s.* Englewood Cliffs, NJ: Prentice Hall, 1983.
   An updated version of the author's pioneering research on the governing class in America, taking account of the phenomenon of the "Reagan Revolution."

Richard Sennett and Jonathan Cobb, *The Hidden Injuries of Class.* New York: Vintage, 1973.
   A pathbreaking work that looks at the social psychological consequences of class inequality.

Theories of Stratification
Michael D. Grimes, *Class in Twentieth-Century American Sociology: An Analysis of Theories and Measurement Strategies.* New York: Praeger, 1991.
   A survey of major contemporary theories of stratification.

CHAPTER EIGHT: Social Class in the United States

CHAPTER OUTLINE

Studying Social Stratification
    Objective Approach
    Reputational Approach
    Subjective Approach

Social Class in the United States
    The Upper Class
    The Upper-Middle Class
    The Lower-Middle Class
    The Working Class
    The Lower Class
    Taking the Sociological Perspective: How Easy Is It to Change Social Class?
    Income Distribution

Poverty
    The Feminization of Poverty
    How Do We Count the Poor?
    Myths About the Poor

Government Assistance Programs
    Controversies in Sociology: Reforming the Welfare System

The Changing Face of Poverty

Consequences of Social Stratification

LEARNING OBJECTIVES

1. Describe and evaluate the methods sociologists use for measuring social class.
2. Describe the characteristics of each of the social classes in the United States in the most commonly used approach.
3. Describe the current distribution of income in the United States.
4. Describe disparities in the rate of poverty among various groups in American society.

5. Describe how the official government poverty index is constructed and identify its weaknesses.

6. Describe and critique four common myths about the poor in the United States.

7. Describe and contrast the various federal programs that provide direct benefits to families or individuals.

8. Compare poverty rates in the United States with those of other industrialized countries.

9. Describe some of the personal and social consequences of a person's position in the class structure.

KEY CONCEPTS

Studying Social Stratification

objective approach: a method in which researchers determine a set number of classes in advance and then assign people to each one based on given criteria.

reputational approach: a method of determining social class that relies on the opinions that community members have of one another.

subjective approach: a method in which individuals are asked to place themselves into one of several class categories.

Social Class in the United States

upper class: a category of people with great wealth, high prestige, and an exclusive lifestyle.

upper-middle class: a category made up of successful business and professional people who generally have a college education, own property, and have a savings reserve.

lower-middle class: a category of lower-ranked professionals, clerical and sales workers, and upper-level manual workers who tend to be high school graduates with modest incomes and some savings.

working class: a category made up of skilled and semiskilled workers, factory employees, and other blue-collar workers who have adequate incomes, but with little left over for luxuries.

lower class: a category of people with little in the way of education or occupational skills who are focused mostly on survival.

Poverty

poverty: a condition in which people do not have enough money to maintain a standard of living that includes the basic necessities of life.

Government Assistance Programs

social insurance: a form of assistance designed to protect people from various economic hazards — retirement, unemployment, disability, etc. — and which is not means-tested.

means-tested assistance: a form of assistance for which people qualify due to low income.

noncash benefits: a form of assistance to individuals and families in which they receive services instead of money.

LECTURE SUGGESTIONS

1. **Studying Social Stratification.** This topic provides a relevant way to reinforce some of the lessons of Chapter 2 on research methods. You can discuss problems of constructing operational definitions, validity, researcher bias, and data collection techniques. Students are likely to remain plugged in here because the discussion all relates to an important real-world issue: How do we know how much inequality there really is?

2. **Problems of Social Mobility.** In the box "Taking the Sociological Perspective," R. Todd Erkel discusses the problems he has faced as a working class interloper in the middle-class world of college and the college-educated. If you have working-class students in your class — or perhaps students from other countries — you may want to solicit their opinions on this subject. How much do their own experiences and perceptions resemble Erkel's? One of the best sociological explanations for this phenomenon is Sennett and Cobb's *The Hidden Injuries of Class,* cited in the Resources for Students section of this manual's Chapter 7. You can get from it many good insights and examples to share with the class.

3. **The Extent of Inequality.** Students often have a difficult time grasping the extent of inequality. If they visualize it at all, they carry around in their heads a bell curve. ("We're all basically middle class.") This view, of course, is greatly mistaken. One good way to help students visualize inequality is Stephen Rose's *American Profile Poster* (see Resources section). This poster, which graphically represents the distribution of income and wealth by occupation, sex, race, and household status, is definitely *not* a bell curve. Although the statistics on which the chart is based are now ten years old, the overall shape of the distribution has not changed significantly (and, to the extent it has, it has become even more extreme in the gap between rich and poor). Economist Paul Samuelson provides a compelling visual metaphor which helps students understand the enormous gap between the rich and the rest of us. If we made an income pyramid out of children's blocks, with each 1"x1" block representing $1,000 of income, the pyramid would be far higher than the Eiffel Tower, but most of us would be within a yard of the bottom. Let that one sink in. Even better, if you've got a picture or slide of the Eiffel (or CNN, etc.) Tower that shows its scale relative to humans, show that to the students while you discuss this metaphor. You're not telling them how to evaluate social inequality, you're making sure that they have an accurate picture of its extent. A good source of easily-digestible critical statistics on social and economic inequality is Steve Brouwer's *Sharing the Pie* (see Resources).

4. **Understanding Poverty.** Most students who have no personal experience with poverty have bought into the myths about the poor perpetuated by grandstanding politicians and/or sensationalized media. In fact, most of this evidence is anecdotal, and often wrong, at least in the aggregate. If possible, invite someone who is officially poor and/or someone who is homeless to come into class and talk about their experiences. Or you might videotape interviews with these people and show them to the class. It shouldn't be hard to find poor people who are bright and fairly articulate. The experience of seeing these people and hearing their stories face-to-face will be a powerful one for many students. The goal, of course, is not to put poor people "on display," but to humanize the category for your students. Check with your local social service agencies for possible guests.

5. **Federal Government Assistance Programs.** Using the information in Table 8-5 and the text, construct a profile of a "typical" recipient of government assistance. Of course they are going to be middle class, and most likely over 65 years old. Read this profile to the class, then discuss stereotypes of government aid recipients. Why do these stereotypes exist? Who benefits from their existence? How are they perpetuated? Tie this in to a discussion of worldwide comparisons. The text states that the United States does fairly well, in comparison with other capitalist industrial countries, in keeping down poverty among the elderly. Yet this country ranks appallingly low, in comparison, on child poverty. Based on Table 8-5,

one could conclude that this is because we have an extensive income transfer program for the elderly, but not much for children. Ask students to try to explain why this is so. Is it likely to change, especially with the aging of the baby boomers?

SUGGESTED ACTIVITIES

1. **Social Class in the Class.** Using Table 8-1 in the text, have each student place themselves in a social class (or more than one if they've had the experience of class mobility). If you think that the subject is too sensitive for the people in your class, you could pass out 3x5 cards and ask students to write their answers anonymously. The cards can then be collected and tallied, with the results written on the board or an overhead transparency. Ask the students to draw conclusions from the data — about themselves, the university, the community, American society, etc.

2. **Understanding Social Classes.** Pair up the students in your class and randomly assign each pair one of the five social classes discussed in the text. Each dyad should write a biography of a "typical" member of their assigned social class. Have the students read and discuss their biographies in class. Later, have each student write about their reactions to the experience. Were their views altered by putting themselves in the place of another? Why or why not?

3. **Visualizing Social Classes.** Talking and reading are not the only ways to learn about a concept. Use an exercise called "living sculpture" to have students visualize the relationship among members of the various social classes. This exercise, which is used in process-oriented counseling (you could learn more about it in that literature or from a counselor who uses the technique, but you don't have to do so to do this exercise), is a relatively non-threatening visual role-playing experience. Divide the students up into groups of five, corresponding to the five social classes discussed in the text (if your class isn't evenly divisible by five, assign the extras as additional working or lower-middle class members in various groups). Tell the students that, after an allotted discussion period, the groups will be asked to come to the front of the room one at a time and create a "living sculpture" that depicts the relationships among the classes as they understand them (or at least one important fact about or dimension of those relationships). Make some basic rules clear before you start: students must exercise a modicum of good taste, and ensure that no one is humiliated or put at risk by the experience. When you challenge student creativity this way, you will be amazed at the really insightful things students do (OK, maybe not always the first time, but if they get comfortable with this kind of participation, they can really learn in unanticipated ways. Make sure that you complement the effort of each group, and discuss their sculpture. Even unimaginative sculptures can be useful — they can tell you what students aren't clear about, or what they misunderstand.

4. **Living in Poverty.** Using Table 8-3 in the text, which lists poverty levels by household size, assign students to live on the appropriate poverty budget for a week (divide the text figures by 52 to get weekly income; try to get more recent figures if they are available). Make sure that students budget for *all* of their expenses, even if they are not normally responsible for paying it, and even if it's not due in the week of the experiment. Even this short time frame should give previously-unaware students a feel for what it's like trying to make ends meet if you're poor. An alternative to this hypothetical exercise is to turn the assignment into field research. Give each student his or her appropriate poverty budget and then tell them they have two weeks (more, if you think it's necessary) to figure out how to meet all of their needs. They must investigate low-income housing, figure out some means of transportation, figure out where and how much it will cost to shop for necessities, check with public agencies about various welfare and subsidy programs, etc. You may want to let students work in pairs on this. If the class is large, check with social service agencies in advance. Most of these agencies are overworked and understaffed, and real clients

should not have to wait for services while agency workers endlessly answer hypothetical questions from students. On the other hand, many of these workers understand (presumably because they've taken sociology courses) that it is in their interest and the interest of their clients for more people to understand the problems they confront. So there are tradeoffs. Before conducting any such field project, make your students thoroughly aware of ethical issues.

RESOURCES FOR INSTRUCTORS

Stephen J. Rose, *The American Profile Poster: Who Owns What, Who Makes How Much, Who Works Where, & Who Lives With Whom.* New York: Pantheon, 1986.

Steve Brouwer, *Sharing the Pie: A Disturbing Picture of the U.S. Economy.* Carlisle, PA: Big Picture Books, 1992.

RESOURCES FOR STUDENTS

Studying Social Stratification
Reeve Vanneman and Lynn Weber Cannon, *The American Perception of Class.* Philadelphia: Temple University Press, 1987.
    A look at popular perceptions in the United States.

Social Class in the United States
Loren Baritz, *The Good Life: The Meaning of Success for the American Middle Class.* New York: Knopf, 1989.
    A look at the assumptions middle-class Americans make about the meaning of success, equality, child-rearing, and freedom.

Income Distribution
Frank Levy, Dollars and Dreams: *The Changing American Income Distribution.* New York: Russell Sage Foundation, 1987.
    An examination of recent trends through the mid-80s.

Poverty
Ken Auletta, *The Underclass.* New York: Vintage, 1982.
    A systematic, journalistic look at the poorest of the poor in America.

Rochelle Lefkowitz and Ann Withorn, eds, *For Crying Out Loud: Women and Poverty in the United States.* New York: Pilgrim Press, 1986.
    A fairly up-to-date examination of "the feminization of poverty."

Jonathan Kozol, *Rachel and Her Children: Homeless Families in America.* New York: Crown, 1988.
    A highly-readable examination of the problem of homelessness in America by a leading social critic.

CHAPTER NINE: Racial and Ethnic Minorities

CHAPTER OUTLINE

The Concept of Race
>Genetic Definitions
>Legal Definitions
>Social Definitions
>*Taking the Sociological Perspective: The "Other" Americans*

The Concept of Ethnic Group

The Concept of Minorities

Problems in Race and Ethnic Relations
>Prejudice
>Discrimination
>>Unprejudiced Nondiscriminators
>>Unprejudiced Discriminators
>>Prejudiced Nondiscriminators
>>Prejudiced Discriminators
>Institutionalized Prejudice and Discrimination

Patterns of Racial and Ethnic Relations
>Assimilation
>Pluralism
>Subjugation
>Segregation
>Expulsion
>*Sociology at Work: Orlando Patterson on Slavery and Freedom*
>Annihilation

Racial and Ethnic Immigration to the United States
>Illegal Immigration
>White Anglo-Saxon Protestants
>African Americans
>Hispanics (Latinos)
>>Mexican Americans
>>Puerto Ricans

Cuban Americans
Taking the Sociological Perspective: What's in a Name?
Jews
Asian Americans
Native Americans

Prospects for the Future

Controversies in Sociology: Is Transracial Adoption Cultural Genocide?

LEARNING OBJECTIVES

1. Critically review the major ways in which race has been defined.

2. Explain the concept of ethnic group.

3. Explain the sociological concept of "minority."

4. Analyze the relationship between prejudice and discrimination.

5. Describe the concept of institutionalized prejudice and discrimination.

6. Distinguish the basic patterns of racial and ethnic relations.

7. Describe the pattern of immigration to the United States.

8. Describe the characteristics of the major racial and ethnic groups in the United States.

KEY CONCEPTS

The Concept of Race
    race: a category of people who are defined as similar because of a number of physical characteristics.

The Concept of Ethnic Group
    ethnic group: a group with a distinct cultural tradition with which its own members identify and which may or may not be recognized by others.

The Concept of Minorities
    minority: a group of people who, because of physical or cultural characteristics, are singled out for differential and unequal treatment, and who therefore regard themselves as objects of collective discrimination.

Problems in Race and Ethnic Relations
    prejudice: an irrationally based negative, or occasionally positive, attitude toward certain groups and their members.

    discrimination: differential treatment, usually unequal and injurious, accorded to individuals who are assumed to belong to a particular category or group.

institutionalized prejudice and discrimination: complex societal arrangements that restrict the life chances and choices of a specifically defined group, in comparison with those of the dominant group.

Patterns of Racial and Ethnic Relations

assimilation: the process whereby groups with different cultures come to share a common culture.

Anglo conformity: the renunciation of other ancestral cultures in favor of Anglo-American behavior and values.

pluralism: the development and coexistence of separate racial and ethnic group identities within a society.

subjugation: the subordination of one group and the assumption of a position of authority, power, and domination by the other.

segregation: the act, process, or state of being set apart.

ghetto: used to describe any kind of segregated living environment.

expulsion: the process of forcing a group to leave the territory in which it resides.

forced migration: the relocation of a group through direct action.

annihilation: the deliberate practice of trying to exterminate a racial or ethnic group.

genocide: a synonym for annihilation.

LECTURE SUGGESTIONS

1. **The Concept of Race.** Race, as noted in the text, is an arbitrary biological concept, but one with real social implications. Perhaps this is nowhere more clear than in transracial families. If possible, try to arrange for a transracial couple and/or a transracial adoptive family to come in and talk to students about their experiences in this society. Also, try to get someone (perhaps someone enrolled in the class?) who defines themselves as biracial or multiracial (the "other" Americans described in the Taking the Sociological Perspective box) to talk with class. You may want to address the validity of racial classification data in social research and social policy.

2. **Social Definition of Race and Ethnicity.** Should cultural identification be on the basis of choice? That is, should people get to choose the cultural community and practices with which they feel most comfortable? The very idea of this, to say nothing of the actual possibility, is uniquely American due to 1) the history of diverse immigration to this country, 2) the pervasive ideology of free choice in this society, and 3) a history of a certain amount of cultural pluralism. An interesting model of conscious choice of ethnic community (having little to do with one's family background, skin color, etc.) may be found in Marge Piercy's utopian novel *Woman on the Edge of Time* (see Resources section). You may want to recount this model to students and get their reactions.

3. **"Minority Groups."** What does it mean when so-called "minority" groups are actually the majority? The term is usually defined from a Caucasian point of view, of course. But non-Caucasians have *always* been a majority in the world. Even in the United States, Caucasians seem on their way to becoming a numerical minority. In California, for instance, so-called minorities will be the numerical majority

sometime after the turn of the century. How will this affect the meaning of the terms? Pose this issue to the class.

4. **Anglo-Conformity.** For years Hollywood stars have changed their names. Today TV, radio and pop music personalities often do likewise. Why is it, however, that the new names are almost always *Anglo* names? Regardless of the intentions of the name changer, the result is the false impression that popular culture is populated only by Anglo people. Make an overhead transparency of the list of celebrity name-changers found in the Resources section at the end of this chapter. Cover both columns, then reveal the names in the left column one at a time. See if the students can guess the person's stage name, listed in the right-hand column. Alternatively, you could make a handout of just the left-hand column and let students work on the names in small groups. Or, if you had to, you could read aloud the names in the left column of the list. See if students recognize 1) who the celebrities actually are, and 2) the pattern of Anglo-conformity. An interesting additional note: Some students may remember that when John Mellencamp started out in the music business, he was known as Johnny Cougar. The story goes that this was not his choice, but rather was dictated by his record company. As soon as Mellenkamp/Cougar had sold enough records to get his way, he insisted on using his real name.

5. **America as a Melting Pot.** Is the United States *really* a melting pot? That is, have the various ethnic identities that are part of the immigrant background been melded into a new synthesis that is a uniquely American identity, or does ethnicity continue to be a salient issue in American culture, especially tensions and conflicts among ethnic groups? Or is the melting pot really an *Anglo-Conformity* pot? (i.e., We are all supposed to melt down and come out looking and thinking Anglo.) Pose this issue to the class, and encourage students to share their own experiences and those of their families.

6. **Slavery and Freedom.** Orlando Patterson's work on slavery and freedom, summarized briefly in the Sociology at Work box in the text, is pathbreaking and provocative. For most students, it is also likely to be a completely different way of conceptualizing the Western tradition. Incorporate some of Patterson's examples into your lecture and get students' reactions. (See Resources section.)

7. **The Ethnic Hierarchy.** Critical Thinking Question #3 in the Study Guide poses the issue of an ethnic hierarchy in America, where the social rankings and locations of ethnic groups correspond roughly to when they came here in large numbers. Ask students for examples of the hierarchy's existence today. (e.g., How many non-WASP U. S. presidents? CEOs of Fortune 500 corporations?) Non-Anglo European groups are just now making it into some positions at the top — e.g., Lee Iacocca at Chrysler.

8. *Teaching Tolerance.* This is a magazine published by the Southern Poverty Law Center and mailed free to educators all over the country. If you aren't on their list, see the Resources section. Although aimed more at elementary and secondary teachers, there are nevertheless many good ideas on multicultural education that can be used by college instructors.

9. **White Supremacist and Hate-Group Activities.** Hard economic times cause hate groups to flourish. Many students are unaware, in spite of the aftermath of the Oklahoma City bombing, of just how vicious and even dangerous some of these groups are. If you can, get some literature from hate groups that operate in your area. Otherwise, a good source of information is the Klanwatch Project of the Southern Poverty Law Center (address in Resource section). Also valuable is the Bill Moyers PBS special on the SPLC's court victory over a hate group in Oregon.

SUGGESTED ACTIVITIES

1. **Racial Attitudes and Experiences.** Assign students to read and report on (orally or in writing) one or more of the vignettes in Studs Terkel's book *Race: How Blacks & Whites Think & Feel About the American Obsession* (see Resources section). Terkel is a master interviewer who has a knack for making his interview subjects comfortable and then letting them tell their own story, usually in revealing detail.

2. **Prejudice.** Ask the class to discuss, in small groups, the question: Is prejudice inevitable? Is it human nature to irrationally pre-judge, or is it actually a personal dysfunction? Under what conditions might prejudice be functional or dysfunctional, for the individual and for society?

3. **Prejudice and Discrimination.** As a way of understanding Merton's typology in the text, describe a situation in a social setting (school, work, neighborhood, etc.) and then ask students, working in small groups, to write a personal statement and behavioral scenario for each of Merton's four categories of people.

4. **Institutionalized Prejudice and Discrimination.** Obtain from the school administration statistics on minority enrollment and, if possible, academic performance at your college or university. Present these figures to your students and ask them to discuss how, if at all, discrepancies in the figures between minority and majority groups could be tied to institutionalized prejudice and discrimination.

5. **Subjugation and Sports Mascots.** Many Native Americans have been highly critical of professional and amateur sports teams that use Native American names and "mascots" — e.g., Redskins, Warriors, Braves, Redmen, Indians. Representatives of these teams often respond to the criticisms by saying that they don't mean the names in a pejorative way — in fact, the names are meant to honor Native Americans. Native Americans reply that we don't "honor" African Americans with team names like the Negroes, Coloreds, Slaves, etc., nor do we "honor" Hispanics with team names like the Spics, Wetbacks, Illegals, etc., and on and on. Why are Native Americans uniquely singled out? Pose this issue to students and have them discuss it. Perhaps they could be assigned to generate a recommendation, with appropriate justification, to the administration of a school or pro team with such a name.

6. **Immigration Restrictions.** Have students debate the need for immigration restrictions in the United States. This includes those mentioned in Table 9-1 in the text as well as any other restrictions students might feel are necessary. Can restrictions be justified? Which ones? On what basis? Who in the class has relatives who might not have been allowed in the country had the proposed restrictions been in place?

RESOURCES FOR INSTRUCTORS

Orlando Patterson, *Freedom: Freedom in the Making of Western Culture.* New York: Basic Books, 1991.

Marge Piercy, *Woman on the Edge of Time.* New York: Fawcett Crest, 1976.

Teaching Tolerance. A biannual publication of the Southern Poverty Law Center. 400 Washington Ave., Montgomery, AL 36104. Free to educators.

Studs Terkel, *Race: How Blacks & Whites Think & Feel About the American Obsession.* New York: The New Press, 1992.

RESOURCES FOR STUDENTS

The Concept of Race

Thomas F. Gosset, Race: The History of an Idea in America. New York: Schocken, 1965.
   A comprehensive history of the doctrine of white supremacy in the United States.

Racial and Ethnic Immigration to the United States

Oscar Handlin, *The Uprooted, 2nd edition, enlarged.* Boston: Little, Brown, 1990.
   The classic history of European immigration to America, updated with recent developments.

Racial and Ethnic Groups in the United States

Frank D Bean and Marta Tienda, *The Hispanic Population of the United States.* New York: Russell Sage Foundation, 1987.
   A comprehensive look at Hispanics today.

Harry H. L. Kitano and Roger Daniels, *Asian Americans: Emerging Minorities.* Englewood Cliffs, NJ: Prentice Hall, 1988.
   A survey of the current status of Americans of Asian origin.

Nicholas Lemann, *The Promised Land: The Great Black Migration and How It Changed America.* New York: Knopf, 1991.
   Although they didn't cross an ocean to get here, African Americans underwent a dramatic immigration experience in this century that transformed them and the country.

Jack Weatherford, *Native Roots: How the Indians Enriched America.* New York: Crown, 1991.
   Shows how a surprising number of American social and cultural institutions and practices are rooted in Native American culture.

CELEBRITY NAME-CHANGERS

Bernie Schwartz . . . . Tony Curtis

Shirley Schrift . . . . Shelley Winters

Allen Stewart Konigsberg . . . . Woody Allen

Cherilyn Sarkisian . . . . Cher

Robert Allen Zimmerman . . . . Bob Dylan

John Henry Deutschendorf, Jr. . . . . John Denver

George Kyriakou Panayiotou . . . . George Michael

Frederick Austerlitz . . . . Fred Astaire

Nathan Birnbaum . . . . George Burns

Emanuel Goldenberg . . . . Edward G. Robinson

Issur Danielovitch Demsky . . . . Kirk Douglas

Natasha Gurdin . . . . Natalie Wood

Stefania Federkiewicz . . . . Stephanie Powers

Melvin Kaminsky . . . . Mel Brooks

Charles Buchinsky . . . . Charles Bronson

Mladen Sekulovich . . . . Karl Malden

Michael Orowitz . . . . Michael Landon

Bernadette Lazzarra . . . . Bernadette Peters

Betty Joan Persky . . . . Lauren Bacall

Mikhail Igor Peschkowsky . . . . Mike Nichols

Ramon Estevez . . . . Martin Sheen

Carlos Estevez . . . . Charlie Sheen

Krekor Ohanian . . . . Mike Connors

Esther Pauline Friedman . . . . Ann Landers

Pauline Esther Friedman . . . . Abigail Van Buren

Margarita Casino . . . . Rita Hayworth

Michaelo Giacomo Vijencio Gubitosi . . . . Robert Blake

Annemaria Italiano . . . . Anne Bancroft

Raquel Tejada . . . . Raquel Welch

William Henry Pratt . . . . Boris Karloff

Jerry Rivers . . . . Geraldo Rivera

CHAPTER TEN: Gender and Age Stratification

CHAPTER OUTLINE

Are the Sexes Separate and Unequal?

Historical Views

Religious Views

Biological Views

Animal Studies and Sociobiology

Genetic and Physiological Differences

Responses to Stress

Sociological View: Cross-Cultural Evidence

What Produces Gender Inequality?

The Functionalist Viewpoint

The Conflict Theory Viewpoint

Gender-Role Socialization

Childhood Socialization

Adolescent Socialization

Sociology at Work: Deborah Tannen: Communication Between Men and Women

Gender Differences in Social Interaction

Gender Inequality and Work

Job Discrimination

Taking the Sociological Perspective: Gender and the Academic Experience

Age Stratification

Composition of the Older Population

Aging and the Sex Ratio

Aging and Race

Aging and Marital Status

Aging and Wealth

Global Aging

Theories of Aging

Disengagement Theory

Activity Theory

Modernization Theory

Future Trends

Controversies in Sociology: Euthanasia: What Is the "Good Death"?

LEARNING OBJECTIVES

1. Contrast biological and sociological views of sex and gender.

2. Describe and illustrate the concept of patriarchal ideology.

3. Compare and contrast functionalist and conflict theory viewpoints on gender stratification.

4. Explain the process of gender-role socialization.

5. Describe the extent and conditions of women's current labor force participation.

6. Describe the ways in which women face discrimination in the world of work.

7. Explain the impact of changes in gender roles in U.S. society.

8. Describe the basic demographic features of the older population in the United States.

9. Compare and contrast theories of aging.

10. Describe important future trends in aging.

KEY CONCEPTS

Are the Sexes Separate and Unequal?

sex: the physical and biological differences between men and women.

gender: the social, psychological, and cultural attributes of masculinity and feminity that are based on biological distinctions.

patriarchal ideology: the belief that men are superior to women and should control all important aspects of society.

ethology: the scientific study of animal behavior.

Gender-Role Socialization

gender-role socialization: the lifelong process whereby people learn the values, attitudes, motivations, and behavior considered appropriate to each sex by their culture.

gender identity: an individual's sense of maleness or femaleness.

Theories of Aging

disengagement theory: states that aging involves an inevitable withdrawal from positions of social responsibility as part of the orderly operation of society.

activity theory: assumes that satisfaction in later life is related to the level of activity the person engages in.

modernization theory: assumes that there is a direct connection between the extent of modernization in a society and the status of the elderly.

baby-boom: the large number of people born between 1946 and 1964.

LECTURE SUGGESTIONS

1. **Gender and Self-Identity.** Tavris (see Resources) reports a study in which Dr. Alice Baumgartner asked a stratified random sample of nearly 2,000 school-age children in Colorado to answer one simple question: "If you woke up tomorrow and found out that you were [the opposite sex], how would your life be different?" The extent to which traditional gender stereotypes were expressed surprised the researcher. Boys were almost universally negative about being girls, but girls had a generally positive response to being boys. It is a real discussion-provoker to read some of the children's verbatim statements to the class. Encourage students in your class to ask children they know the same question (most students won't need much encouragement!). A question based on this study appears in the Critical Thinking section of this Study Guide chapter.

2. **Patriarchal Ideology.** Reference is made to Letty Cottin Pogrebin's view of patriarchal ideology in the Study Guide exercises. I like to organize at least a portion of my lecture around the two phrases she says sum up the ideology — Boys Are Better and Girls Are Meant To Be Mothers — and, with the students' active participation, find aspects of our culture that confirm the ideology, and aspects that run counter to it.

3. **Gender-Role Socialization.** An excellent source on this subject is Pogrebin's *Growing Up Free* (see Resources for Students below). The narrative is accessible and well-informed; the extensive citations provided in the endnotes show that the author did her homework in the appropriate academic literature.

4. **Adolescent Gender-Role Socialization.** Popular music is an important source of group identification for adolescents. Bring in some examples of songs or music videos that contain gender stereotypes and discuss them with the class. What does it mean to feature these messages so prominently in our culture?

5. **Language and Gender Stereotypes.** Because language shapes the way we think, it affects the way we interact with one another. And our language is laden with gender stereotypes. Pogrebin gives a number of examples. For more examples and a more extensive critique, see Spender, *Man Made Language* (see Resources section).

6. **Language and Gender.** One of the most important ways in which gender inequality is reinforced, I feel, is the use of the generic male ("mankind, man, he, his, him, chairman, Congressman, fireman, etc.). To demonstrate the built-in bias of this practice, try to go a whole class period using the generic female (Does that concept seem weird to you? Why?). Don't explain to students — at least not until near the end of class. Dismiss any objections prior to then as trivial: "Come on now, you know what I mean." Students are bound to have a variety of reactions, and the debriefing should be a learning experience for everyone.

7. **Job Discrimination.** Try to get a woman with a professional or managerial job to come in and talk to the class about the "glass ceiling" in organizations that permits women to rise only to a certain point. The ceiling is even more significant for women of color.

8. **Gender and Organizations.** Rosabeth Moss Kanter showed, in *Men and Women of the Corporation* (see Resources) that jobs make people. More specifically, she argued that many of the characteristics we ascribe to females in the workplace are actually derived to a greater extent from the types of jobs people

do. The book is a rich treasury of information, examples, and strategies for positive change.

9. **Housework.** In the Resources section at the end of this chapter is a potential handout on housework in contemporary industrial/postindustrial society. Point out to students that it happens in many different ways, but the uniting factor is that it's "women's work." See how many examples of each category students can come up with. One excellent analysis of a mundane task is DeVault's *Feeding the Family* (see Resources). Lest students think that the movement of women into the labor force has changed who is responsible for housework, quote the data and some examples from Hochschild's *Second Shift* (see Resources).

11. **Euthanasia.** Invite a guest speaker or panel of speakers to address the "right to die." Suggestions for participants include a medical ethicist from your own faculty or a local hospital, an ICU nurse or doctor, a lawyer familiar with living will and assisted death statutes in your state.

SUGGESTED ACTIVITIES

1. **Patriarchal Ideology.** Divide the class into small groups and have them each come up with 3-5 of their best examples of Pogrebin's dimensions of patriarchal ideology, then have the class share them. If you want to get into policy, have the class then discuss what, if anything, can be done to change these messages.

2. **Biological vs. Sociological Explanations of Gender Differences.** Have students write about and/or discuss the implications of biological explanations of gender differences and gender behavior (e.g., rape, emotional expression). What does it mean for the kind of society we have, and for the individuals within it?

3. **Gender-Biased Perceptions of Behavior.** Bring to class a videotape of an infant whose sex is not readily apparent and is dressed in gender-neutral clothes (if you don't have such tapes yourself, nearly any new parent will be happy to oblige). Play the tape for your students and tell them you want them to watch for cognitive and social development clues. During the discussion phase, student disagreement over the gender of the baby should immediately become obvious — do some call it *he* and some call it *she*? Ask why they feel one way or the other. More significant than what the infant actually *did* will be the students' gender-shaded *perceptions* of the baby.

4. **Theories of Aging.** Assign students to interview 3-5 people over 65 years of age about their activities and their attitudes toward aging. Then, in small groups, have students evaluate the theories of aging discussed in the text in light of their data.

5. **Impact of an Aging Population.** The text provides data to show that the proportion of older Americans is beginning to grow rapidly. Have students brainstorm five positive and five negative social changes they see coming about in our society as a result of this demographic transformation.

RESOURCES FOR INSTRUCTORS

Marjorie L. DeVault, *Feeding the Family: The Social Organization of Caring as Gendered Work.* Chicago: University of Chicago Press, 1991.

Arlie Hochschild, *The Second Shift: Working Parents and the Revolution at Home.* New York: Viking, 1989.

Rosabeth Moss Kanter, *Men and Women of the Corporation.* New York: Basic Books, 1977.

Dale Spender, *Man Made Language.* London: Routledge & Kegan Paul, 1980.

Carol Tavris, with Dr. Alice I. Baumgartner, "How Would Your Life Be Different If You'd Been Born A Boy?" *Redbook* February 1983, pp. 92-95.

RESOURCES FOR STUDENTS

Are the Sexes Separate and Unequal?
Bettina Aptheker, *Tapestries of Life: Women's Work, Women's Consciousness, and the Meaning of Daily Experience.* Amherst: University of Massachusetts Press, 1989.
> Weaves stories, poems, oral histories, paintings, and essays into an examination of women's unique experience. The author aims to suggest the ways of thinking that arise out of the dailiness of women's lives.

What Produces Gender Inequality?
Beth B. Hess and Myra Marx Feree, *Analyzing Gender: A Handbook for Social Science.* Beverly Hills, CA: Sage, 1987.
> A compendium of current social science research on gender: theory, stratification, sexuality, religion, the family, politics, and more.

Gender-Role Socialization
Letty Cottin Pogrebin, *Growing Up Free: Raising Your Child in the 80's.* New York: Bantam, 1980.
> A comprehensive, research-based examination of childhood gender-role socialization, with suggestions on how to avoid stereotypes.

Gender Inequality and Work
Ann Helton Stromberg and Shirley Harkess, *Women Working: Theories and Facts in Perspective, Second Edition.* Mountain View, CA: Mayfield, 1988.
> A reader that examines all facets of women and work in contemporary U.S. society.

Age Stratification
Arlie Russell Hochschild, *The Unexpected Community: Portrait of an Old Age Subculture.* Berkeley: University of California Press, 1978.
> A pioneering ethnographic study of 43 older people living in a single apartment building in San Francisco. Readable, insightful, and useful for presenting the point of view of older people.

Future Trends in Age Stratification
Alan Pifer and Lydia Bronte, eds., *Our Aging Society: Paradox and Promise.* New York: Norton, 1986.
> An outcome of the Carnegie Corporation's The Aging Society Project, this volume examines, from a social science perspective, the important ways in which an aging population is likely to transform American society.

HOUSEWORK

DEFINITION OF HOUSEWORK

women's unpaid/low-paid work to reproduce the labor force
— physically, psychologically, and socially

TYPES OF HOUSEWORK

Occupational — traditional family reproduction tasks; unpaid, not in the labor force. Increasingly involves a great deal of unpaid consumption work

Industrial — the housework industry: domestics, janitors, "cleanin' women without faces"

Institutional — the Pink Collar Ghetto: clerical, sales, and service jobs; the reserve army of the unemployed or sporadically employed

Organizational — mostly unpaid social and emotional work within organizations

Structural — paid and volunteer labor that mitigates exploitation and alienation: social work, United Way, Junior League, women's shelters, community festivals, etc.

CHAPTER ELEVEN: Marriage and Alternative Family Lifestyles

CHAPTER OUTLINE

The Nature of Family Life

Functions of the Family

Regulating Sexual Behavior

Patterning Reproduction

Organizing Production and Consumption

Socializing Children

Providing Care and Protection

Providing Social Status

Family Structures

Defining Marriage

Romantic Love

Marriage Rules

Marital Residence

Mate Selection

Age

Race

Religion

Social Status

The Transformation of the Family

Changes in the Marriage Rate

Childless Couples

Changes in Household Size

Women in the Labor Force

Sociology at Work: Arlie Hochschild on Working Parents

Family Violence

Divorce

Divorce Laws

Child-Custody Laws

Remarriage and Stepfamilies

Alternative Lifestyles

The Growing Single Population

Single-Parent Families

Cohabitation

Homosexual and Lesbian Couples

The Future: Bright or Dismal?

Controversies in Sociology: Are Fathers Necessary?

LEARNING OBJECTIVES

1. Explain the functions of the family.

2. Describe the major variations in family structure.

3. Define marriage and describe its relationship to the phenomenon of romantic love.

4. Describe the various rules governing marriage.

5. Explain the ways in which mate selection is not random.

6. Explain the impact of industrialism on the modern family.

7. Summarize recent changes in the family as an institution.

8. Explain the impact of recent changes in divorce and child custody laws.

9. Describe the various alternative lifestyles in contemporary American society.

KEY CONCEPTS

The Nature of Family Life

household: people who share the same living space.

incest taboo: a norm that forbids sexual intercourse among closely related individuals.

nuclear family: a married couple and their children.

polygamous family: a set of nuclear families linked by multiple marriage bonds, with one central individual married to several spouses.

polygynous family: a family in which the central individual is a male and the multiple spouses are females.

polyandrous family: a family in which the central individual is a female and the multiple spouses are males.

extended family: a family that includes other relations and generations in addition to the nuclear family.

patrilineal system: a situation in which the generations are tied together through the males of a family.

matrilineal system: a situation in which the generations are tied together through the females of a family.

bilateral system: a situation in which descent passes through both females and males of a family.

patriarchal family: a situation in which most family affairs are dominated by men.

matriarchal family: a situation in which most family affairs are dominated by women.

Defining Marriage

marriage: the socially recognized, legitimized, and supported union of individuals of opposite sexes.

divorce: the breakup of marriage.

romantic love: a phenomenon characterized by idealization of a loved one, the notion of a one and only, love at first sight, love winning out over all, and an indulgence of personal emotions.

family of origin: the family in which a person was born and raised.

family of orientation: the family in which a person was raised.

family of procreation: the family created by marriage.

endogamy: a situation in which people are directed to marry within certain social groups.

exogamy: a situation in which individuals are required to marry someone outside their culturally defined group.

monogamy: the situation in which a person is allowed only one spouse at a time.

multiple marriages: the situation in which an individual may have more than one spouse.

marital residence rules: norms that govern where a newly married couple settles down and lives.

patrilocal residence: a requirement that a new couple settle down near or within the husband's father's household.

matrilocal residence: a requirement that a new couple settle down near or within the wife's mother's household.

bilocal residence: a situation in which a newly married couple can choose to live with either the husband's or the wife's family of origin.

neolocal residence: a situation in which a newly married couple may choose to live virtually anywhere.

homogamy: the tendency to choose a spouse with a similar social and cultural background.

The Transformation of the Family

companionate marriage: marriage based on romantic love.

marriage rate: the proportion of the total population marrying.

no-fault divorce: a situation in which, in principle, the financial aspects of marital dissolution are to be based on equity, equality, and economic need rather than fault- or gender-based role assignments.

joint custody: a legal situation in which parental decision-making authority is given equally to both parents after a divorce.

stepfamilies: families that include children from parents' previous marriages.

Alternative Lifestyles

   cohabitation: a situation in which unmarried couples live together.

LECTURE SUGGESTIONS

1. **Family Structures.** There have always been a variety of ways to form families, and a variety of shapes to family structure. Today, however, it seems we are inventing/exploring even more options. With the breakdown of the extended family through social and geographical mobility, a great deal of pressure has been put on the isolated nuclear family. And with a higher divorce rate, we have more single parents. Out of necessity, people are exploring new family types: "fictive kinship" arrangements like surrogate grandparents, aunts and uncles; "big brother and big sister" mentoring relationships with young people; various housesharing arrangements; peer groups of friends as surrogate family. If you can, put together a panel of people from various types of families (some of them may even be students in your class) and have them articulate for your students their own personal quests for family. Note how these alternative family structures go about fulfilling the six functions of the family.

2. **Defining Marriage.** Tischler observes that "there is no doubt that 'couplehood,' as either a reality or an aspiration, is as strong among gay men and lesbian women as it is among heterosexuals." In this light, ask students to analyze the definition of marriage Tischler gives in this chapter. Except for the phrase "individuals of opposite sexes," why couldn't this definition apply to many gay and lesbian couples? Likewise with the four ways in which marriage differs from other unions, according to Tischler. Some may object that the text seems to imply that marriage legitimates only biological offspring. We know, however, that in nearly every society, adopted children are legitimized as well. So, aside from religious objections (and, admittedly, these will be strong on the part of some students), why don't we socially legitimate as marriages relationships between partners who meet all the criteria but happen to be of the same sex?

3. **Romantic Love and Marriage.** As Tischler notes, these two are so tied together in our culture that it may be difficult to get students to see them as only arbitrarily connected. But it is useful to get them to do so. Romance is often equated with infatuation. Have students help you generate a list of the dysfunctions of trying to build a long-term relationship on infatuation (What happens when the glitter fades?) Next have students help you generate a list of the non-romantic functions of marriage. Are these important enough to warrant serious and careful (i.e., relatively non-emotional) analysis and implementation? Since marriage is a socially-legitimated phenomenon, what interest does society have in people developing marriage partnerships that are based on more than physical attraction or infatuation?

4. **Marriage Rules.** In the text, Tischler quotes Marvin Harris to the effect that "some form of polygamy occurs in 90 percent of the world's cultures." Harris says that the reason that, in most of these societies, only a minority of people practice it is that only a minority can afford it. We live in an affluent society, but it is one of the 10 percent that does not allow polygamy. Ask students why they think this is so. Should we allow polygamy? What would be the functions and dysfunctions of doing so? How would it change our society? Note: don't let students automatically assume that polygamy means polygyny; it can mean polyandry, too, and probably would in a society with an emphasis on equality between the sexes.

5. **Transfer of Functions from the Family.** Have students help you draw up a list of functions that have been transferred out of the family to other institutions over the last 30 years. What are the positive and negative consequences of this transfer of functions?

6. **Change in Household Size.** Average American household size today is less than half of what it was 200 years ago. In concert with the class, draw up a list on the board or on an overhead transparency of the positive and negative consequences of this change. Try to get the students to really stretch their sociological imaginations and look at economic, political and cultural as well as social factors.

7. **Working Parents.** Research shows that American households, while smaller, have more income earners in them than ever before, and those income earners are spending more time earning income. The group that has increased its hours of work the most is working parents with preschool-age children. In terms of childhood socialization, these are precisely the people who can least afford to work extra hours. On the other hand, the costs of starting and maintaining a household with children make it necessary to work more and more hours. What are the implications of this? What has to change?

8. **Family Violence.** Wherever you are, there must be some sort of support program for victims of family violence (if there isn't, start one!). Invite some knowledgeable staff members and/or clients of the agency or program to come in and give students information on the etiology of the problem and the *modus operandi* of abusers. Ask the class to discuss the causes of family abuse, especially gender socialization.

9. **Divorce.** Pose the following questions to the class and collectively work through the answers. Should we worry about having a high divorce rate? Does it suggest a social and cultural failure? Does society have a legitimate stake in the success of interpersonal relationships? If so, what can be done to protect that stake? Divorce, as the Study Guide suggests, is a topic that provides a good application of the distinction between ideal and real norms.

10. **Regulating Marriage and Divorce.** What interest does the state really have in regulating relations between consenting adults? Culturally, it seems important for humans to have rituals celebrating and formalizing certain relationships. But why make it part of the legal system (unless the individuals are minors, or there are minor children involved)? What would be the implications of doing away with marriage and divorce laws and procedures? (Anything requiring adjudication could be handled under existing civil statutes. This is sure to be a discussion-provoker in class.

11. **Alternative Family Types.** Adoptive families face a number of issues and challenges beyond those faced by more traditional type families. Invite a panel of adoptive parents and children (some may be enrolled in your class, or colleagues) to address the class on these unique issues, showing how the adoptive family is both the same and different than other families.

12. **Qualifications of Child-Rearers.** Does society have a legitimate interest in regulating who can have and raise children? Just because two people are biologically capable of creating a child, should they automatically be allowed to raise that child? (We all know horror stories where the answer is a resounding "NO!") Adoptive parents have to go through a screening process in which their motives and capabilities are closely examined. Should we do this for biological parents as well? One barrier to this in our society is the idea of children as the private property of their parents. But isn't the next generation of a society *everyone's* business, in a sense? And doesn't everyone suffer when resources have to be devoted to dealing with dysfunctional individuals? If being antisocial is preventable, then why don't we prevent it? What would be the implications, for society and for individuals, of changes to accomplish this?

SUGGESTED ACTIVITIES

1. **The Mythical Family of the Past.** You can often find the "old-fashioned-family shows" from the 1950s and 1960s (*Leave It to Beaver, Ozzie and Harriet, Father Knows Best,* etc.) on cable TV or even in video stores. Bring a taped segment of one of these shows in to your class and ask students to discuss what is *missing* from these shows — on their own terms, to say nothing of contemporary issues.

2. **Functions of the Family.** Write the six functions of the family on the board, an overhead transparency, or on a handout given to students. Working in small groups, have them try to come up with as many different ways of meeting each function as they are familiar with. Then have each group share with the class as a whole. This exercise should make students more aware of the variety of ways in which these functions can be carried out.

3. **Comparison of Family Structures.** Assign students to view a variety of television shows that portray families. The shows should be from different eras and should portray families as different social class levels (access to cable TV is a necessity). It is probably easier to divide the class into small groups and let each group decide how they will divide up the assignment. Have students write about what they observe and/or discuss it in class.

4. **Mate Selection and Homogamy.** The American high school is one of the prime vehicles to create and reinforce homogamy. In small groups (where they will likely be more comfortable with the topic), ask students to discuss the dating practices of their high school. What were the norms of homogamy? How were people made aware of them? How were these norms enforced? What happened when the norms of homogamy were violated?

5. **Mate Selection.** As an exercise, ask students to write down their ideal criteria for mate selection, regardless of their current or past marital status. As they discuss these criteria in small groups, they should note patterns of commonality and difference. Students who have practical experience in deviating from these criteria may want to share that experience, to the extent they are comfortable with it.

RESOURCES FOR STUDENTS

The Nature of Family Life
Christopher Lasch, *Haven in a Heartless World: The Family Besieged.* New York: Basic Books, 1979.
>   A penetrating critique of the way that the social sciences and the helping professions have understood and treated the family in this century.

Defining Marriage
Philip Blumstein and Pepper Schwartz, *American Couples.* New York: Morrow, 1983.
>   A revealing study based on interviews with hundreds of different kinds of couples.

The Transformation of the Family
Arlene S. Skolnick and Jerome H. Skolnick, eds, *Family in Transition, 6th ed.* Boston: Little, Brown, 1988.
>   A comprehensive reader on changes in the modern family and family life.

Alternative Lifestyles
Maxine Baca Zinn and D. Stanley Eitzen, *Diversity in Families, 2nd ed.* New York: Harper and Row, 1990.
>   A look at widely divergent family lifestyles.

CHAPTER TWELVE: Religion

CHAPTER OUTLINE

The Nature of Religion

The Elements of Religion

Ritual and Prayer

Emotion

Belief

Organization

Taking the Sociological Perspective: Human Societies and the Concept of God

Magic

Major Types of Religions

Supernaturalism

Animism

Theism

Monotheism

Abstract Ideals

A Sociological Approach to Religion

The Functionalist Perspective

Satisfying Individual Needs

Social Cohesion

Establishing Worldviews

Adaptations to Society

The Conflict Theory Perspective

Organization of Religious Life

The Universal Church

The Ecclesia

The Denomination

The Sect

Millenarian Movements

Aspects of American Religion

Widespread Belief

Secularism

Ecumenism

Major Religions in the United States
Protestantism
Catholicism
Judaism
Islam
Social Correlates of Religious Affiliation
Controversies in Sociology: Are Religious Cults Dangerous?

LEARNING OBJECTIVES

1. Explain the nature of religion and differentiate it from magic.

2. Define the basic elements of religion.

3. Differentiate among the major types of religion.

4. Describe the functions of religion according to the functionalist perspective.

5. Explain the conflict theory perspective on religion.

6. Describe the basic types of religious organization.

7. Describe important aspects of contemporary American religion.

8. Describe the major religions in the United States.

KEY CONCEPTS

The Nature of Religion
religion: a system of beliefs, practices, and philosophical values shared by a group of people that defines the sacred, helps explain life, and offers salvation from the problems of human existence.

profane: things that are knowable through common, everyday experiences.

sacred: things that are awe-inspiring and knowable only through extraordinary experience.

rituals: patterns of behavior or practices that are related to the sacred.

prayer: a means for individuals to address or communicate with supernatural beings or forces.

Magic
magic: an active attempt to coerce spirits or to control supernatural forces.

Major Types of Religions
supernaturalism: belief in the existence of nonpersonalized supernatural forces that can and often do influence human events.

mana: a diffuse, nonpersonalized force that acts through anything that lives or moves.

religious taboo: a sacred prohibition against touching, mentioning, or looking at certain objects, acts, or people.

animism: belief in inanimate, personalized spirits or ghosts of ancestors that take an interest in and actively work to influence human affairs.

theism: belief in divine beings — gods and goddesses — who shape human affairs.

polytheism: belief in a number of gods.

monotheism: belief in the existence of a single god.

abstract ideals: focus on the achievement of personal awareness and a higher state of consciousness through correct ways of thinking and behaving, rather than manipulating spirits or worshiping gods.

A Sociological Approach to Religion

totem: an ordinary object that has become a sacred symbol to and of a particular group or clan.

revitalization movements: religious movements that stress a need to return to the traditional religious values of the past.

alienation: the process by which people lose control over the social institutions they themselves invented.

Organization of Religious Life

universal church: includes all the members of a society within one united moral community.

ecclesia: a church that shares the same ethical system as the secular society and has come to represent and promote the interest of the society at large.

denomination: a religious group that tends to limit its membership to a particular class, ethnic or religious group.

sect: a small group that adheres strictly to religious doctrine that often includes unconventional beliefs or forms of worship.

millenarian movements: movements that typically prophesy the end of the world, the destruction of all evil people and their works, and the saving of the just.

Aspects of American Religion

secularized: a society that is less influenced by religion.

ecumenism: the trend among many religious communities to draw together and project a sense of unity and common direction.

KEY THINKERS/RESEARCHERS

Émile Durkheim: a pioneer in the sociology of religion; first distinguished between the sacred and the profane and discussed religion's role in promoting social cohesion.

Rodney Stark and William Bainbridge: discussed the relationship between magic and Christianity.

Sigmund Freud: said that religion was irrational, but helpful to the individual in coming to terms with impulses that induce guilt and anxiety.

Max Weber: discussed, in *The Protestant Ethic and the Spirit of Capitalism,* how the ideology of Calvinism had influenced the development of capitalism.

Marvin Harris: showed that the Hindu belief in the sacredness of cows is a positive strategy for adapting to the environment in India and therefore quite rational.

Karl Marx: argued that religion is a tool that the upper classes use to maintain control of society and to dominate the lower classes.

LECTURE SUGGESTIONS

1. **The Nature of Religion.** There is probably no more emotional subject they you can discuss in class than religion. This is due to the fact that most religions contain significant non-rational elements — mysteries or, literally, "leaps of faith." Yet you can turn this to your advantage by asking students to reflect on just that non-rational aspect. In Western society, most aspects of our lives are dominated by rationality, and we demand rational explanations for phenomena. Yet, in the area of religion, many Americans not only accept non-rational approaches, but they vehemently oppose anyone who tries to apply rationality to thinking about religion. Ask students, using their best sociological imaginations, to try and explain this. Answers based on religions dogma, teaching or interpretation, while very important to many individuals, are not acceptable as sociological answers here.

2. **The Elements of Religion.** Pose to the class the metaphor of football as America's secular religion. Then go through each of the elements and show how it is present, and how the profane has been transformed into the sacred (e.g., Superbowl Sunday as our national holyday of obligation). As an alternative, you may want the students to come up with examples. While you must be careful of student sensitivities about religion (see #1 above), the comparison is sociologically legitimate, and if done tastefully, can produce some real sociological thinking among students.

3. **Major Types of Religions.** Invite someone from a nontraditional religion in America (Hindu, Buddhist, Baha'i, Shinto, Islam, Native American, etc.) to talk to the class about their religious views. Ask the class to draw parallels with traditional religions.

4. **Types of Religions.** Many anthropological documentaries, and some feature films, show religious practices, even as an ancillary part of the presentation. If you can locate and show one or more of these to the class, you can make students' awareness of similarities and differences more acute.

5. **Social Cohesion as a Function of Religion.** As Tischler notes in the text, Durkheim believed that when people worship supernatural entities, they are really worshipping their own society. Ask students what they think of this point. Can they envision a society with no religion? How would it be different?

6. **The Protestant Ethic and Capitalism.** The popularization of Weber's argument has led to its trivialization — the Protestant Reformation occurred, and then out of religious conviction Protestants invented capitalism. Weber's argument was more complex, and it may be worthwhile making that clear to students. A resource that leads to a more balanced view — i.e., how capitalism caused Protestantism as well as vice versa — is R.H. Tawney's easily readable paperback (see Resources section).

7. **Religion as "the opiate of the masses."** This quote of Marx's is probably the single most misquoted and taken-out-of-context statement in his entire work. I would urge you to read the statement in context, which is only about five paragraphs in a relatively obscure early work of Marx's (see citation of one source in the Resources section). From this you will learn, I think, at least two things: First, Marx said that religion was the *opium* of the people, not the *opiate*. A small difference, but one that is significant, because it makes the argument more clinical. That is, opium was used then as it is now both to anesthetize physical pain and to escape a painful social reality. When the whole context of Marx's statement is read, he seems to be saying — and this is the second point — that no one would oppose narcotics for people in pain. But, given the long-run deleterious effects of those narcotics, wouldn't it be better to eliminate the source of the pain? For Marx, of course, the source of pain was capitalism. So Marx's statement is not as much anti-religion as it is anti-capitalism. Read the whole thing for yourself and then read it to students. Or duplicate and distribute it. If you distribute it to the class, you may want to do so early in your discussion of religion with no identification on it. Just have students read it and see what they think, without pre-judging it on the basis of their knowledge or stereotypes of the author.

8. **Sects, Cults, and Millenarian Movements.** There are a variety of good movies and books on this subject. Expose students to some of this material and then ask them to put themselves in the place of one of the members of a group studied. Can they see how the world looks to this imagined other? Can they understand why the (to outsiders bizarre) behavior makes sense? Working on these questions should get students thinking more sociologically, rather than psychologically, about these groups.

SUGGESTED ACTIVITIES

1. **The Sacred and the Profane.** Ask students, working in small groups, to come up with a list of cultural objects or practices that have moved from the sacred to the profane or from the profane to the sacred. If students need prompting, mention Native American cultures (a rich source of examples: e.g., Thunderbird, Dakota, headdress, turquoise, peyote) or various subcultures.

2. **Magic.** Tischler quotes Stark and Bainbridge to the effect that magic's respectability has decreased in contemporary society. Ask students to discuss the extent to which this is true, and to compile a list of magical practices in modern society. If students need prompting, ask them to think about the phenomenon of "miracles," both sacred and secular.

3. **Types of Religions.** Assign students to visit religious services of a religion with which they are unfamiliar or less familiar, or to watch "the electronic church" on television. What are the primary messages being conveyed? How are these messages similar to, and different from, the religious messages with which they are more familiar?

4. **Functionalist vs. Conflict Theory Perspectives on Religion.** Divide the class into teams and have them debate the two perspectives. Encourage the debaters to use specific examples (not in the text) that the team members have generated.

5. **Organization of Religious Life/Religions in the United States.** Conduct an anonymous survey of the class in which students indicate what, if any, religious organization they identify with. Compile the results and classify them according to the categories in the text (and any others that make sense in terms of the data). Discuss how representative students think the class is of the larger society. Why is it or why isn't it?

RESOURCES FOR INSTRUCTORS

R.H. Tawney, *Religion and the Rise of Capitalism.* New York: Mentor, 1954.

Karl Marx, "Introduction to a Contribution to a Critique of Hegel's Philosophy of Law" in Karl Marx and Frederick Engels, *Collected Works, Vol. 3.* New York: International Publishers, 1975.

RESOURCES FOR STUDENTS

The Nature of Religion
Phillip E. Hammond, ed., *The Sacred in a Secular Age: Toward Revision in the Scientific Study of Religion.* Berkeley: University of California Press, 1985.
> A contemporary social science look at all aspects of the sacred in modern life. In addition to a wide range of topics, it is comparative and cross-cultural.

Major Types of Religion
Ninian Smart, *The World's Religions.* Englewood Cliffs, NJ: Prentice Hall, 1989.
> An examination of the major religions of the world, including the geographic areas in which each is dominant.

A Sociological Approach to Religion
Keith A. Roberts, *Religion in Sociological Perspective.* Homewood, IL: Dorsey, 1984.
> A comprehensive, well-written introduction to the sociological aspects of religion.

Organization of Religious Life
Rodney Stark and William Sims Bainbridge, *The Future of Religion: Secularization, Revival, and Cult Formation.* Berkeley: University of California Press, 1985.
> An examination of current trends in religious belief and organization.

Aspects of American Religion
Jeffrey K. Hadden and Anson Shupe, *Televangelism: Power and Politics on God's Frontier.* New York: Henry Holt, 1988.
> A sociological analysis of television evangelists, their followers, and their impact on American politics and culture.

CHAPTER THIRTEEN: Education

CHAPTER OUTLINE

Education: A Functionalist View

Socialization

Cultural Transmission

Academic Skills

Innovation

Taking the Sociological Perspective: Will Computer Games Transform Education?

Child Care

Postponing Job Hunting

The Conflict Theory View

Social Control

Screening and Allocation: Tracking

The Credentialized Society

Sociology at Work: Jonathan Kozol on Unequal Schooling

Issues in American Education

Unequal Access to Education

Students Who Speak English as a Second Language

High School Dropouts

Violence in the Schools

Standardized Testing

The Gifted

Controversies in Sociology: Is There Gender Bias in the Classroom?

LEARNING OBJECTIVES

1. Describe the manifest and latent functions of education according to the functionalist view.

2. Explain the nature of education from the conflict theory view.

3. Explain the causes and effects of racial segregation in the public schools.

4. Identify issues relating to students who speak English as a second language.

5. Discuss the extent to which high school dropouts are a social problem.

6. Discuss the issue of standardized testing.

7. Evaluate the idea of special programs for gifted students.

KEY CONCEPTS

Education: A Functionalist View

   cultural transmission: the process in which major portions of a society's knowledge are passed from one generation to the next.

The Conflict Theory View

   hidden curriculum: the social attitudes and values taught in school that prepare children to accept the requirements of adult life and to "fit into" the social, economic, and political statuses the society provides.

   tracking: the stratification of students by ability, social class, and various other categories.

Issues in American Education

   de jure segregation: a form of racial separateness based on laws prohibiting interracial contact.

   de facto segregation: a form of racial separateness resulting from residential housing patterns.

   white flight: the exodus of large numbers of white Americans from the central cities to the suburbs.

KEY THINKERS/RESEARCHERS

   National Commission on Excellence in Education: their report, A *Nation at Risk*, instigated the current educational reform movement.

   R. Rosenthal and L. Jacobson: conducted a famous study that demonstrated the powerful effect of the self-fulfilling prophecy in school.

   Samuel Bowles and Herbert Gintis: they argue that educational success is more likely to be determined by possession of the appropriate personality traits than by merit or intelligence.

   James Coleman: author of a 1966 survey of 645,000 children that demonstrated substantial class and race differences in educational achievement and opportunity.

LECTURE SUGGESTIONS

1. **The Purposes of Education.** Conduct an anonymous survey in class in which each student is asked to write about why he or she is attending college. Collect and compile the surveys and share the data with the students. Ask students to categorize the various explanations, making their criteria explicit. Then ask them to normatively evaluate the reasons. Are these reasons appropriate? By what standards?

2. **Cultural Transmission: Bilingual Education.** Have part or all of your lecture translated into a foreign language. If you can do it yourself, all the better; if not, one of your colleagues who is fluent in another language will probably be willing to help you, especially when you tell them why you're asking. If you don't speak the language fluently, you'll have to have it marked phonetically so that you can say it out loud. Don't worry about having perfect pronunciation — it's not crucial to this exercise. Make English translations for half the students in your class, and copies of a literal transcription of your lecture in the foreign language for the other half. Shuffle the two types together and randomly pass the sheets out at the start of class. Without any further explanation, begin lecturing in your foreign language. The students

who speak the language or who have the "crib notes" can follow along fairly easily, even if your pronunciation isn't perfect (see, I told you!). The rest of the students, of course, are out of luck. Therefore you will undoubtedly hear howls of protest. "This isn't fair. How are we to know what you're talking about?" Explain to them that you've given them your own lecture notes, which is certainly more than you're required to do. If they don't understand them, it's their job to get some help translating them. Since many other students clearly do understand, you can't spend valuable class time going over the material again. (And how many times have students heard *that* before?) Depending on your class and local conditions, you may want to call the experiment to a halt at this point. Or you may want to take it to the next level, and really hang tough, refusing to give the students with the foreign language versions any more help, waiting until the next class period to discuss the issue. In any event, be sure to debrief the students, discussing the nature of the exercise, and assuring them that no student will be penalized as a result of this exercise. But the point is, isn't it true that people who aren't very familiar with English penalized? Aren't they required, on a regular basis, to get translation help? Is it ethnocentric to say to them, "Too bad. Just learn English." I am quite sure that you will generate more sympathy for ESL (English as a second language) students as a result of this exercise.

3. **Academic Skills.** Much has been made recently of an apparent decline in the basic skills of many students graduating from American high schools. Explore with the class the possible explanations for this phenomenon. Does it have to do mainly with *what* is or isn't being taught, *how* it is being taught, the *context* in which it is being taught, and/or the students' understandings of *why* they are in school in the first place and *where* their education is likely to lead?

4. **Functionalist vs. Conflict Theory Perspectives on Education.** After students have read and discussed the material on these perspectives, schedule a panel of school principals or other administrators and ask them to discuss what they are trying to accomplish in their schools. Encourage students to ask pointed, but fair questions.

5. **Social Control in Education.** Bring to class a copy of the Bill of Rights. As you move through each of the ten amendments, ask students to comment on the extent to which that freedom exists in elementary and secondary school. What will be discovered is that almost none of them do. Ask students for their reactions. Is it ironic that school supposedly prepares students for citizenship, but doesn't let them practice it?

6. **Education and Freedom.** An excellent film to show on education is "Summerhill," which examines the school of the same name founded by A.S. Neill. A residential school in England, Summerhill was begun with children expelled from other schools and classified as delinquents. It operates on the principles of respect for self and others and freedom. The school is self-governing; everyone, students and faculty alike, has just one vote. The film shows weekly self-governing meetings, and contains revealing interviews with Neill and a number of students. Most college students cannot believe that such a school could exist anywhere except in fantasy. Therefore it is useful to show the movie (or have them read sections of his book — see Resources section) in order to stimulate their imaginations with regard to educational structure. Also in the Resources section are citations for a book compiling the debate over the principles of Summerhill, and a biography of Neill and Summerhill.

7. **The "Gifted."** What does it really mean to be "gifted." There are a variety of problems with the determination of such a group of people. Tischler mentions the problem of gender, race, class, and disability biases. Also, what about the apparent existence of multiple intelligences? Are they all taken into account when determining "giftedness"? Many people assume that the way to deal with giftedness is to separate the "gifted" from everyone else. An alternative would be to have the "gifted" work with the less-talented, and help them to progress. The gifted would learn, too, because you always learn

125

something better by having to teach it to someone else.

SUGGESTED ACTIVITIES

1. **Cultural Transmission in Education.** Robert Fulghum wrote a popular book a few years ago called *All I Really Need to Know I Learned in Kindergarten*. You may want to read to the students the section where he recounts the major messages learned in kindergarten that would also be valuable in adult life (e.g., "Don't hit people. Don't take things that aren't yours. Share. Play fair.") Ask students to list the messages they remember from elementary and secondary school, and compare it with Fulghum's list. How do the two lists differ? Further, ask students to classify the messages on their list as positive or negative ("do" vs. "don't"). Does one category clearly outweigh the other? Why?

2. **Academic Skills.** What constitute appropriate academic skills? Share with your students Bloom's Taxonomy of Cognitive Skills (see Resources section). Which cognitive skills are fostered by the pedagogical techniques of the "back-to-basics" movement? Which cognitive skills are most important for functioning in a complex society characterized by rapid social change? How should these skills be fostered and developed in higher education? Have the students apply higher-level cognitive skills in their discussion and recommendations.

3. **Innovation and Education.** According to the functionalist argument, generating innovation is an important task of education. In contemporary American society, large-scale or expensive research projects occur largely at the behest of major economic actors — large corporations and government bureaucracies. How does this shape the process of innovation? Have students write about innovations they think are *not* occurring because funding cannot be obtained to explore them.

4. **Self-esteem and education.** Research on both child development and education indicate that self-esteem is important to a child's ability to learn. Yet a recent Gallup Poll showed that while 80 percent of all kindergartners have high self-esteem, only 40 percent of fifth graders, and 5 percent of high school seniors did so. Ask students to generate hypotheses about why this finding was obtained.

5. **Tracking.** In small groups, have students discuss their experiences with tracking — for good or ill — during their years of elementary and secondary education. In the larger group, see what generalizations they can develop. To what extent does the college or university they are now attending represent a form of tracking?

6. **Equal Access to Quality Education.** Given the existence of *de facto* segregation and the wide disparity in the funding of schools documented by critics like Kozol, how should equal opportunity for acquiring a quality education be ensured? Or is this goal unrealistic? Or unacceptable? Have students work in groups to generate solutions/recommendations. If the students' work merits further attention, send it (with their permission) to your local school board and the state legislature.

7. **Standardized Testing.** Illustrate the cultural bias in standardized testing by administering a test (as an exercise, of course) that is biased toward a particular group — e.g., an African-American- or Hispanic-oriented IQ test. I once took an IQ test (again, as an exercise) where the questions were based entirely upon knowledge of farming practices and implements (something which, at one time, nearly everyone had). As a bonafide city boy I didn't do too well. You ought to be able to find such a test in the literature or put one together yourself without too much problem. After giving students the results back, have them discuss their experiences with standardized tests.

RESOURCES FOR INSTRUCTORS

Benjamin S. Bloom (ed.), *Taxonomy of Educational Objectives: The Classification of Educational Goals.* New York: D. McKay, 1974.

Robert Fulghum, *All I Really Need to Know I Learned in Kindergarten: Uncommon Thoughts on Common Things.* New York: Villard Books, 1988.

Ray Hemmings, *Children's Freedom: A.S. Neill and the Evolution of the Summerhill Idea.* New York: Schocken, 1972.

A.S. Neill, Summerhill: A Radical Approach to Child Rearing. New York: Hart Publishing, 1960. (to be republished in a revised edition as *Summerhill School: A New View of Childhood,* edited by Albert Lamb. New York: St. Martin's, 1993.)

Summerhill: For and Against. New York: Hart Publishing, 1970.

RESOURCES FOR STUDENTS

Perspectives on Education
Stanley Aronowitz and Henry A. Giroux, *Education Under Siege: The Conservative, Liberal and Radical Debate Over Schooling.* South Hadley, MA: Bergin and Garvey, 1985.
    Despite its subtitle, this book is really a radical analysis of the purpose and possibilities of schooling.

Kathleen P. Bennett and Margaret D. LeCompte, *How Schools Work: A Sociological Analysis of Education.* New York: Longman, 1990.
    A comprehensive look at education in the United States today from a sociological perspective.

Ira Katznelson and Margaret Weir, *Schooling for All: Class, Race, and the Decline of the Democratic Ideal.* New York: Basic Books, 1985.
    Critical of conventional conservative, liberal, and radical perspectives on education, the authors argue that American schools have been shaped by both capitalism and democracy, and that the democratic ideal embodied in them is currently undermined by class and race inequality.

Issues in American Education
Paulo Freire, *Pedagogy of the Oppressed.* Translated by Myra Bergman Ramos. New York: The Seabury Press, 1970.
    A philosopher of education describes his method for teaching — and empowering — illiterate adults through dialogue about their life conditions.

Ivan Illich, *Deschooling Society.* New York: Harper and Row, 1970.
    A classic work that argues that education has become too bureaucratic, and the solution is to move learning out into the community by creating democratic, grass-roots, person-to-person "learning webs."

CHAPTER FOURTEEN: Political and Economic Systems

CHAPTER OUTLINE

Politics, Power, and Authority

Power

Political Authority

    Legal-Rational Authority

    Traditional Authority

    Charismatic Authority

Taking the Sociological Perspective: The Importance of Presidential Concession Speeches

Government and the State

Functions of the State

    Establishing Laws and Norms

    Providing Social Control

    Ensuring Economic Stability

    Setting Goals

    Protecting Against Outside Threats

The Economy and the State

Capitalism

    Private Property

    Freedom of Choice

    Freedom of Competition

    Freedom from Government Interference

The Marxist Response to Capitalism

Command Economies

Socialism

The Capitalist View of Socialism

Types of States

Autocracy

Totalitarianism

Democracy

Democracy and Socialism

Democratic Socialism

Functionalist and Conflict Theory Views of the State

Political Change

Institutionalized Political Change

Rebellions

Revolutions

   Political Revolutions

   Social Revolutions

The American Political System

The Two-Party System

Voting Behavior

African Americans as a Political Force

Hispanics as a Political Force

A Growing Conservatism

Special-Interest Groups

   Lobbyists

   Political Action Committees

Controversies in Sociology: Do the Media Have Too Powerful a Role in Elections?

LEARNING OBJECTIVES

1. Distinguish between authority and coercion.

2. Compare and contrast Weber's three types of legitimate authority.

3. List and explain the basic functions of the state.

4. Analyze the basic features of capitalism.

5. Describe the Marxist critique of capitalism.

6. Explain the relationship between capitalism, socialism, and democratic socialism.

7. Describe autocratic and totalitarian forms of government.

8. Describe the basic features of political democracy.

9. Contrast the functionalist and conflict theory views of the state.

10. Describe the basic mechanisms of political change.

11. Describe the major features of the American political system.

KEY CONCEPTS

Politics, Power, and Authority

   politics: the process by which power is distributed and decisions are made.

   power: the ability of a person or group to get their way, even in the face of resistance or opposition.

authority: power that is regarded as legitimate by those over whom it is exercised.

coercion: power that is regarded as illegitimate by those over whom it is exerted.

legal-rational authority: a form of authority derived from the understanding that specific individuals have clearly defined rights and duties to uphold and implement rules and procedures impersonally.

traditional authority: a form of authority rooted in the assumption that the customs of the past legitimate the present.

charismatic authority: a form of authority derived from a ruler's ability to inspire passion and devotion among followers.

Government and the State

the state: the institutionalized way of organizing power within territorial limits.

autocracy: a form of government in which ultimate authority rests with one person, who is the chief source of laws and the major agent of social control.

aristocracy: a form of government in which a select few rule.

The Economy and the State

economy: the social institution that determines how a society produces, distributes, and consumes goods and services.

capitalism: an economic system based on private ownership of the means of production, and resource allocation through the market.

laissez-faire capitalism: the view that government should stay out of business affairs.

mixed economy: a combination of free-enterprise capitalism and governmental regulation of business and provision of social welfare programs.

command economy: an economic system in which the government makes all the decisions about production and consumption.

socialism: an economic system in which the government owns the sources of production and sets production and distribution goals.

Types of States

totalitarian government: a situation in which one group has virtually total control of a nation's social institutions.

totalitarian socialism: a situation in which the government, in addition to almost total regulation of all social institutions, owns and controls all major means of production and distribution.

communism: another name for totalitarian socialism.

totalitarian capitalism: a situation in which the government, while retaining control of social institutions, allows private ownership of the means of production.

fascism: another name for totalitarian capitalism.

democracy: a political system operating under the principles of constitutionalism, representative government, majority rule, civilian rule, and minority rights.

constitutionalism: a situation in which government power is limited by law.

representative government: the situation in which the authority to govern is achieved through, and legitimized by, popular elections.

electorate: those citizens eligible to vote.

civilian rule: a situation in which every qualified citizen has the legal right to run for and hold an office of government.

dictatorship: a totalitarian government in which all power rests ultimately in one person.

democratic socialism: a convergence of capitalist and socialist economic theory in which the state assumes ownership of strategic industries and services, but allows other enterprises to remain in private hands.

Political Change

rebellion: an attempt — typically through armed force — to achieve rapid political change not possible within existing institutions.

revolution: an attempt to change a society's previously existing structure rapidly and dramatically.

political revolution: a relatively rapid transformation of state or government structures that is not accompanied by changes in social structure or stratification.

social revolution: a rapid and basic transformation of a society's state and class structures.

The American Political System

lobbying: attempts by special-interest groups to influence government policy.

political action committees: a special-interest group concerned with very specific issues that usually represents corporate, trade, or labor interests.

KEY THINKERS/RESEARCHERS

Max Weber: developed the sociological definitions of power and authority.

Plato: constructed a philosophical argument for aristocracy as the best form of government.

Aristotle: argued that power should be centered in the middle class and that the rights and duties of the state should be defined in a legal constitution.

Adam Smith: regarded as the father of modern capitalism; discussed many of the basic premises of this system.

Karl Marx: a severe critic of capitalism who argued that it was based on alienation and exploitation.

LECTURE SUGGESTIONS

1. **Types of Authority.** Take an example of an important state action (e.g., declaring war on another country; making significant changes in American institutions) and ask students how the action would be explained and carried out differently by legal-rational, traditional, and charismatic leaders.

2. **Capitalism and Mixed Economies.** The world economic system is enormously complex, and understanding its mechanisms and nuances can be quite daunting to a nonspecialist. One good resource that allows one to discuss the world economy in a literate way is Epping's *A Beginner's Guide to the World Economy* (see Resources section).

3. **The Marxist Response to Capitalism.** The gross inadequacies of the totalitarian communist systems of Eastern Europe that led to their recent collapse does not necessarily vitiate Marx's critique of capitalism. What the alternatives are to capitalism (or whether there should be any) and what its problems are seem to be two separate — or at least separable — issues. Regardless of the proposed alternatives, students should know the most powerful critique of the system in which they live. Then they will be able to make more informed judgments about it. To that end, there is in the Resource section at the end of this chapter a handout on the Marxist view of capitalism that I share with my class. Citations to explain things further include Lekachmann and Van Loon, Bowles and Edwards, and Mandel — all listed in one of the Resources sections.

4. **Market vs. Command Economies.** If you have access to anyone with expertise on life in Eastern Europe under the Communist regime, set up a panel in which you pair them up with a social worker, counselor, or someone else who is familiar with the downside of living in a market society. This should give students a fresh way of looking at their own society.

5. **Democracy and Socialism.** There are a wide variety of theorists and activists in the United States who argue that, because of our long democratic traditions, *real* democratic socialism — i.e., a society that is fully democratic *and* fully socialist — has a good chance to be a viable reality here. Foremost among these theorists/activists are Albert and Hahnel (see Resources section — also see their work in the edited volume by Shalom mentioned in this section as well).

6. **Functionalist vs. Conflict Theory Views of the State.** Pose various examples of government expenditures to the class and ask them to contrast functionalist and conflict theory explanations as a way of better understanding the theories as well as the role of the state.

7. **The American Two-Party System.** Bring in to class, through lectures, guest speaker, or supplementary readings, information on the parliamentary system used by all but three of the world's industrial democracies. Then, working with students, develop a chart in which you assess the plusses and minuses of the two types of systems. Pay particular attention to the issue of minority voices and positions and their ability to be heard.

8. **Special-Interest Groups.** Invite a panel of lobbyists (your college or university or its association probably have one) to class to discuss what they do and why they do it. Alternatively, have state or federal legislators come in and explain how they understand the role of lobbyists and Political Action Committees and how they personally relate to them. If this live panel is not desirable or possible, have students draw up a list of relevant questions and then contact their own legislators for answers. Personal contact is best, but everyone ought to at least be able to get a written response (especially if the request doesn't look like a form letter).

SUGGESTED ACTIVITIES

1. **Authority vs. Coercion.** When does the exercise of power become illegitimate? Provide students with a number of institutional contexts (e.g., the federal or state governments, the administration of your college or university) and ask them to discuss and list the types of actions that would be defined as coercive and lead to de-legitimation. Be sure you get them to state the basis on which the acts would be defined as coercive.

2. **Plato vs. Aristotle on the Ideal Form of the State.** Divide the class into three teams: the Platonists, the Aristotelians, and the jury. Then stage a debate between the Platonists and the Aristotelians over the proper form of the state in contemporary American society. Remind students that this is not a historical debate; they are to address how Plato's or Aristotle's solution would be best for *today*. At the conclusion of the arguments, the jury deliberates. The jury can choose Plato's or Aristotle's argument, or, having heard the other ideas debated, they can come up with some different ideas of their own.

3. **Democracy.** Hand out a list of the characteristics of democracy listed in the text. Ask students, in small groups, to evaluate the extent to which these features are viable in American society. Next, have them discuss the extent to which these features are absent from our economic system. Then, similar to Critical Thinking Question #3, ask them how they reconcile these conflicting conditions of democracy.

4. **Voting Behavior.** Conduct an anonymous poll in the class in which you ask students if they voted in the most recent election for which they were eligible to vote. Why or why not? Compile the results and present them to the class. This should provoke a vigorous discussion on the meaning and mechanics of democracy.

RESOURCES FOR INSTRUCTORS

Michael Albert and Robin Hahnel, *Socialism Today and Tomorrow.* Boston: South End Press, 1981.

Michael Albert and Robin Hahnel, *The Political Economy of Participatory Economics.* Princeton, NJ: Princeton University Press, 1991.

Samuel Bowles and Richard Edwards, *Understanding Capitalism: Competition, Command, and Change in the U.S. Economy.* New York: Harper & Row, 1985.

Randy Charles Epping, *A Beginner's Guide to the World Economy: Seventy-one Basic Economic Concepts the Will Change the Way You See the World.* New York: Vintage Books, 1992.

Ernest Mandel, *An Introduction to Marxist Economic Theory.* New York: Pathfinder Press, 1970.

RESOURCES FOR STUDENTS

The Economy and the State
Phillip Corrigan, Harvie Ramsay, and Derek Sayer, *Socialist Construction and Marxist Theory: Bolshevism and its Critique.* New York: Monthly Review Press, 1978.
>A critique of command economies from a Marxist point of view.

Robert Lekachman and Borin Van Loon, *Capitalism for Beginners.* New York: Pantheon, 1981.
>Don't let the comic-book format fool you — this is a serious, substantive discussion and critique of how capitalism works, presented in an easily accessible way.

Stephen Rosskamm Shalom, ed., *Socialist Visions.* Boston: South End Press, 1983.
>Presents, in a dialogue format, visions of how a populist socialist society could be created in the United States. Leading thinkers discuss transformations in six areas of life, followed by discussion and debate from others.

Political Change
Samuel Bowles, David M. Gordon, and Thomas E. Weisskopf, *After the Wasteland: A Democratic Economics for the Year 2000.* Armonk, NY: M.E. Sharpe, 1990.
>A critique of the workings of the U.S. economy over the last 40 years and recommendations for change.

The American Political System
Frances Fox Piven and Richard A. Cloward, *Why Americans Don't Vote.* New York: Pantheon, 1987.
>A discussion of why so few Americans vote compared with other democracies. Also suggests what can be done about it.

A MARXIST ANALYSIS OF CAPITALISM

Capitalism = a mode of production (way of working) characterized by:

1) the Market *
2) Private Ownership of the Means of Production **
3) Wage Labor ***

*   Implies the exchange of goods in search of profit; also implies the existence of commodities (goods and services produced for the purpose of exchange). In fact, capitalism is the first mode of production in history where commodity production is generalized (i.e., the majority of human needs are met through market exchange).

**   In theory, all individuals possess the right to own means of production; in fact, capitalism destroys private property for the majority of the population and concentrates ownership in the hands of a few.

*** Those who own no property must exchange the one commodity they do possess, their *ability to work* (labor-power), in the market in return for a wage. In capitalism, this exchange, which seems on the surface, to be fair, is always arranged such that in carrying out the labor service part of the bargain the worker is exploited.

DRIVING FORCES OF CAPITALISM*
Competition
•among capitalists: by a desire to protect their own markets/profits
                     by a multiplicity of decision centers
                     by lack of overall planning and regulation
•among workers in their attempts to access and protect labor markets and levels of consumption

Class Conflict
•the producing class attempts to limit/eliminate exploitation and coercion
•the ruling class struggles to maintain its authority and control

*both factors encourage technological innovations as well as induce their rapid acceptance

TENDENCIES (LAWS OF MOTION) OF CAPITALISM
1) Tendency Toward Concentration and Centralization of Capital
Causes
•inevitable scheming by capitalists to "corner the market" (includes enlisting government
    support through favorable laws and regulations)
•shakeout caused by periodic crises — firm size increases, creating barriers to entry
    (exacerbated by the increasing required investment in technology)
•attempts to survive and regulate class conflict (higher returns go to those capitalists best able to
    invest in controlling technologies/management schemes)

Manifestations
•increasing *concentration* = increasing *in*tensive control within industries and industrial sectors
    e.g., horizontal and vertical monopolies/oligopolies

136

•increasing *centralization* = increasing *ex*tensive control across sectors and society
    e.g., conglomerates; ownership of wealth by a limited few

2) Tendency of the Rate of Profit to Fall

Causes

•realization crisis (underconsumption)
    — competition and class conflict generate constant pressure for technological innovation, which increases productivity
      result: more produced, fewer people employed; therefore there is a decrease in demand
    — each capitalist wants to keep the wages of *their* workers as *low* as possible, but those of *other capitalists'* workers as *high* as possible
      result: due to competition, wages wind up staying low
      thus high levels of demand can't be sustained; capitalists are stuck with overproduction

•disproportionalities created by lack of coordination of the market
    — i.e., uneven development occurs across firms, sectors, and regions due to the contradictory plans of a multiplicity of individual firms

•the rising organic composition of capital ($^c/_v$ —higher proportion of fixed capital to wages) depresses the *rate* of profit ($^s/_{c+v}$ — denominator grows at the expense of the numerator)
    — profits can only be generated by paying living workers wages (v) and not by the use of machines and raw materials (c), which are the embodiment of past labor and can only transfer their value to the final product (depreciation)

Possible offsetting strategies

•direct public resources to boost consumption (Keynesianism)
•implement some form of national economic planning
•increase the rate of exploitation ($^s/_v$) by:
    √ lowering wages (including runaway plants)
    √ increasing absolute surplus value (length and/or intensity of workday)
    √ increasing relative surplus value (productivity)
•expand production into product lines and places (e.g., colonies) with a low organic composition of capital
discover/create highly-profitable new markets and products
    e.g., railroads, autos, Cabbage Patch dolls, Nintendo, home computers

3) Tendency Toward Crisis

Causes

•persistent realization crisis (underconsumption)
•wage squeeze on profits: decreasing unemployment results in rising wages
    thus capital goes on strike until it can get a better profit deal
•uneven development (economic, social, geographic) inevitably results in shortages and irrationalities

Implications

•crises take place on ever higher and more serious levels, with ever more at stake
•state intervention is required (Keynesianism), but according to the existing "rules of the game" (don't interfere with private ownership, wealth, and decisionmaking too much) it cannot ultimately be effective

137

4) Tendency Toward Uneven Development

= disproportionalities among industries, firms, workers, and geographic areas

Causes
- search for profitable investment opportunities "on the margin"
- lack of coordination of the market, caused by the contradictory plans of individual firms
- differential investment in labor as a control strategy
- competitive protection of privileges in production and consumption

Results
- absolute immiseration for some
    - e.g., Third World peasants and workers
    - e.g., environmental destruction in both the developed and underdeveloped countries
- relative immiseration for many (i.e., increasing gap between what *could be* and what *is*)
    - e.g., deskilling of the labor force (more service jobs; increasingly "brainless" work)
    - e.g., alienation, commodity fetishism

BASIC CONTRADICTION OF CAPITALISM:

Contradiction = irresolvable conflict; a problem that cannot be solved within the parameters of the existing system

Progressive Socialization but Continued Private Appropriation

i.e., an ingrained conflict between the forces and social relations of production
- capitalism produces enormous possibilities for human social development, but then systematically inhibits them because the "rules of the game" don't permit their fulfillment
    - e.g., fundamental irrationality of people denied goods (especially food, housing, health care) under conditions of a constant crisis of *over*production
    - e.g., exhausting overwork for a few; little or no work for many
    - e.g., degradation and stupefication of work in spite of the development of technologies which potentially allow for tasks to be unified into a meaningful whole
    - e.g., systematic uneven development of people, places, and communities resulting in unnecessary inequalities

138

CHAPTER FIFTEEN: Population and Demography

CHAPTER OUTLINE

Population Dynamics
> Fertility
> Mortality
> Migration

Theories of Population
> Malthus's Theory of Population Growth
> Marx's Theory of Population Growth
> Demographic Transition Theory
>> Applications to Industrial Society
> A Second Demographic Transition
>> Pronatalist Policies

Current Population Trends: A Ticking Bomb?

Determinants of Fertility
> *Sociology at Work: Paul Ehrlich on the Population Explosion*
> Average Age of Marriage
> Breast-Feeding
> Infant and Child Mortality
> Gender Preferences
> Benefits and Costs of Children
> Contraception
> Income Level
> Education of Women
> Urban or Rural Residence

Problems of Overpopulation
> Predictions of Ecological Disaster
> Sources of Optimism
> *Controversies in Sociology: Why Isn't the U.S. Infant Mortality Rate Lower?*

LEARNING OBJECTIVES

1. Explain the current Chinese population policy.

2. Describe the phenomenon of exponential growth.

3. Define the three major components of population change.

4. Contrast the Malthusian and Marxist theories of population.

5. Summarize the demographic transition model and explain why there might be a second demographic transition.

6. Discuss the determinants of fertility and family size.

7. Discuss problems of overpopulation and possible solutions.

8. Describe the "doomsday model" of ecological disaster and its critique.

KEY CONCEPTS

Population Dynamics

demography: the study of the size and composition of human populations as well as the causes and consequences of changes in these factors.

fecundity: the physiological ability to have children.

fertility: the actual number of births in a given population.

crude birthrate: the number of annual births per 1,000 people in a given population.

fertility rate: the number of annual births per 1,000 women of childbearing age in a given population.

mortality: the frequency of deaths in a population.

crude death rate: the annual number of deaths per 1,000 people in a given population.

age-specific death rate: the number of deaths per 1,000 people at specific ages.

infant mortality rate: the number of children who die within the first year of life per 1,000 live births.

life expectancy: the average number of years that a person born in a given year can expect to live.

migration: the movement of populations from one geographical area to another.

emigration: the phenomenon that occurs when part or all of a population leaves an area.

immigration: the phenomenon that occurs when population enters a geographical area.

internal migration: movement of populations within a nation's boundaries.

Theories of Population

preventive checks: in Malthus's theory, practices that limit reproduction.

positive checks: in Malthus's theory, events that limit the population by causing death.

demographic transition theory: the concept that societies, as they industrialize, pass through four stages of population change, from high fertility and mortality to low fertility and mortality.

Problems of Overpopulation

dependency ratio: the number of people of nonworking age in a society for every 100 people of working age.

KEY THINKERS/RESEARCHERS

Thomas Malthus: a pioneer in the study of population, he believed that population growth is linked to certain natural laws.

Karl Marx: argued that industrial capitalism was the cause of overpopulation.

utopian socialists: people who advocated a reorganization of society to eliminate poverty and other social evils.

Warren Thompson: developed the demographic transition model.

Club of Rome: a group of scientists, academics, and businesspeople who have predicted worldwide economic and ecological collapse.

Paul Ehrlich: one of the first to warn against the catastrophic consequences of unchecked population growth.

LECTURE SUGGESTIONS

1. **Chinese Population Policy.** Many students have heard or read something about Chinese population policy; mostly their perception is that it is a harshly repressive feature characteristic of a totalitarian government. However, by just changing the phrasing of it, without altering the policy itself, it suddenly sounds pretty all-American. Or at least something that is not at all foreign to us. The trick is that, rather than calling the penalties for having more than one child "punishments," turn the whole description of the policy on its head and discuss the voluntary economic rewards for having one child (or no children) by saying that "the Chinese policy allows people to have as many children as they can afford." Clearly there is no absolute prohibition on Chinese couples having three or more children. Nor is the government taking children away from couples who do have them. The government's position is that the socially responsible thing to do is to have only one child, as the society as a whole cannot afford more. If, however, you want to have more, you are free to do so if you can find a way to pay for it. Ask the students how different this is, really, from the situation in the United States. Don't most couples make decisions about how many children to have based on their family economic situation? (Hopefully you have already dispelled the myth of the "welfare queens" having babies in order to get rich when you covered Chapters 8 and 9 of the text.) Aren't there financial penalties, in the United States, for having "too many" children? Don't we leave it up to individual families, pretty much, to figure out on their own how to pay for their children? So, how different are we from China???

2. **The Societal Dysfunctions of China's One-Child Policy.** Like most other societies, China is characterized by patriarchy, where males are given higher value and exercise more power and privilege

than females. Male children are generally more highly valued because they carry on the family name, wealth, and traditions, while girls must be married off, at some expense, to other families. In this context, one outcome of China's one-child policy is a dramatic growth in female infanticide: if a family is only going to have one child, then it "makes sense" to want a boy; if a family "by accident" has a girl, she is often disposed of. This practice is officially condemned by the government; yet it is difficult to take action against it. The results are troubling. For one thing, soon China's sex ratio among young adults will be heavily skewed toward toward males. While this may be good for the population problem (fewer women available to bear children), it will have profound social and cultural impacts. (For one thing, it may greatly increase the power of the now-limited-numbers of women.) This is a good example of the interdependence of social institutions. The Chinese government tried to change one aspect of the family institution in isolation from economic and cultural practices. The result will be problematic. Discuss this issue with students. Can they identify any policies of our government that are the functional equivalent of this? (Example: the former welfare policy that prevented mothers from having men live with them, which contributed to the subversion of the African-American family.)

3. **Population Dynamics.** An excellent source for relatively current population data as well as clear, easy-to-understand explanations of demographic concepts (with examples), is the Population Reference Bureau (see Resources section). In particular, they publish a *Population Handbook* which is a good, inexpensive ready reference, and Population Data Sheets for the United States (data for every state and region on all major measures) and for the world (data on every country in the world). These are excellent sources of supplementary lecture materials.

4. **Life Expectancy.** Have students examine Table 15-2 in the text (and any other information you bring in — see #3 above). It is clear that children born today in many Third World countries will have only two-thirds or less of the life expectancy of children born in the United States and other developed industrial nations. Should we be concerned about this? If so, what forms should that concern take? Students are probably used to viewing years of life as a form of wealth, but aren't they? What does this say about the gap between rich and poor countries, and the ability of the poor countries to close that gap?

5. **The Demographic Transition.** This model is a useful way to compare the differing experiences of the developed industrial countries and the underdeveloped countries. I have found though, that many students find the model confusing initially. So it is probably useful for you to go through it carefully, asking students for explanations and additional illustrations for each stage. It may also help if you prepare another graphic, similar to Figure 15-2 in the text (perhaps an overlay), which shows that the Third World is effectively "stuck" at Stage Two of the model.

6. **A Second Demographic Transition.** Ask students if they find it ironic that, while countries like China are desperately trying to rein in population growth by limiting births, other countries, mostly European, are actually *encouraging* births through pronatalist policies. Does this reflect a failure on the part of the pronatalists to think globally? Is it absurd? Is it racist? or at least extremely ethnocentric — "*We* should have lots of babies, but *you* should slow down."

SUGGESTED ACTIVITIES

1. **Population Dynamics.** Have students plot some exponential functions so that they can get a feel for just how quickly the numbers mount in the rapid increase phase. If students have access to computer labs with appropriate software, then this is an option. But so is plain old graph paper, which you can distribute to students in class. Try to generate functions that have social meaning to the students — perhaps you want to have them assist in this.

2. **Theories of Population.** Divide students into teams and have them develop arguments about the population problem as Marxists or Malthusians. In a twist to the usual procedure, however, ask each team to come up with hypothetical demographic statistics to describe themselves — i.e., what are the social characteristics of those who support each of these theorists?

3. **Current Population Trends.** Have students debate Critical Thinking Question #5 in the Study Guide, with one side arguing that the "ticking bomb" is to be found in the rapidly increasing population of Third World countries, and the other side arguing that the "population problem" is found mainly in the slow-growing, but more-deadly-to-the-planet industrialized countries of Europe, North America, and Japan.

4. **Determinants of Fertility.** Have students do in class the exercise for Learning Objective #6 in the Study Guide. It involves developing a strategy for advising an underdeveloped country how to most effectively lower their fertility rates and decrease average family size. This would make a good writing assignment as well as an in-class exercise. You might also point out to students that this is the kind of applied sociology and consulting that real-life professional sociologists do.

5. **The U.S. Infant Mortality Rate.** In the box "Controversies in Sociology" in this chapter, Nicholas Eberstadt argues that the only way to lower the infant mortality rate is through behavioral interventions with parents. Ask students to look at Table 17-3, which suggests that there are other types of illness prevention strategies. Ask students to come up with structural-level interventions and compare them with Eberstadt's solutions. Ask students to evaluate the potential effectiveness of each strategy. You may even want to do this as a debate.

RESOURCES FOR INSTRUCTORS

Population Reference Bureau, Inc. 1875 Connecticut Ave. N.W., Suite 520, Washington, D.C. 20009-5728. (202) 483-1100. Call or write for a catalog.

(see next page)

RESOURCES FOR STUDENTS

Population Dynamics

Elizabeth Croll, Delia Davin, and Penny Kane, *China's One-Child Family Policy.* London: Macmillan, 1985.

> Discusses the roots and consequences of China's policy.

Arthur Haupt and Thomas T. Kane, *Population Handbook, 3rd edition.* Washington, D.C.: Population Reference Bureau, 1991.

> Defines, explains, and illustrates, in an easily-accessible way, all the basic terms that demographers use. Includes a glossary and a guide to sources of population data.

Theories of Population

Karl Marx and Friedrich Engels, *Marx and Engels on Malthus,* edited by Ronald L. Meek. New York: International Publishers, 1954.

> Gathers together scattered comments from throughout their works that present a critique of Malthusianism.

George F. McCleary, *The Malthusian Population Theory.* London: Faber and Faber, 1953.

> Faithfully details Malthus's basic ideas on population.

Current Population Trends: A Ticking Bomb?

Medea Benjamin and Andrea Freedman, *Bridging the Gap: A Handbook to Linking Citizens of the First and Third Worlds, 2nd edition.* Cabin John, MD: Seven Locks Press, 1990.

> Describes churches, schools, communities, and local governments attempting to deal with world poverty and hunger through people-to-people projects. Includes a resource guide to organizations.

Mary Mederios Kent and Kimberly A. Crews, *World Population: Fundamentals of Growth, 2nd edition.* Washington, D.C.: Population Reference Bureau, 1990.

> A workbook filled with graphics and explanations for world population trends. Includes an appendix with basic demographic data for every country in the world.

Frances Moore Lappé and Joseph Collins, *World Hunger: Twelve Myths.* San Francisco: Food First Books, 1986.

> Written in an easily-accessible style and thoroughly documented, this work presents the argument that hunger is created by unjust social structure, not overpopulation.

CHAPTER SIXTEEN: Urban Society

CHAPTER OUTLINE

The Development of Cities
>   The Earliest Cities
>   Preindustrial Cities
>   Industrial Cities

Urbanization
>   Classification of Urban Environments
>   The Structure of Cities
>>   Concentric Zone Model
>>   Sector Model
>>   Multiple Nuclei Model

The Nature of Urban Life
>   *Gemeinschaft* and *Gesellschaft*
>   *Sociology at Work: William H. Whyte on the Role of the City Center*
>   Mechanical and Organic Solidarity
>   Social Interaction in Urban Areas
>   Urban Neighborhoods
>   Urban Decline
>   Homelessness
>   *Controversies in Sociology: How Many of the Homeless Are Mentally Ill?*

Future Urban Growth in the United States
>   Suburban Living
>   Exurbs

LEARNING OBJECTIVES

1.   Describe the phenomenon of urbanization, historically and in today's world.

2.   Contrast preindustrial and industrial cities.

3.   Distinguish among the different terms that are used to describe urban environments.

4.   Contrast alternative models of urban structure.

5.   Contrast the experience of rural community with the varieties of city life.

6.   Describe the cycle of urban decline and possible countertrends.

7. Describe the current phenomenon of homelessness in American cities.

8. Describe trends in urban growth in the United States.

KEY CONCEPTS

The Development of Cities

preindustrial cities: cities established before the Industrial Revolution.

industrial cities: cities established during or after the Industrial Revolution.

Urbanization

city: a unit that typically has been incorporated according to the laws of the state within which it is located.

urbanized area: an area that contains a central city and the continuously built-up, closely settled surrounding territory that together have a population of 50,000 or more.

urbanization: the process whereby a population becomes concentrated in a specific area because of migration patterns.

urban population: inhabitants of an urbanized area and places with a population of 2,500 or more.

metropolitan area: an area that has a large population nucleus and adjacent communities that are economically and socially integrated into that nucleus.

metropolitan statistical area (MSA): counties that have at least one central city or urbanized area with a population of 50,000 or more, as well as any outlying counties that have close economic and social ties to the central urbanized area.

primary metropolitan statistical area (PMSA): a large, urbanized county or cluster of counties with a population of 1 million or more.

megalopolis: a metropolitan area with a population of a million or more that encompasses two or more smaller metropolitan areas.

consolidated metropolitan statistical area (CMSA): the federal government's name for a megalopolis.

human ecology: the theoretical attempt to explain human communities by the dynamics of plant and animal communities.

concentric zone model: a model of urban development in which distinct, class-identified zones radiate from a central business district.

sector model: a model of urban development in which groups establish themselves along transportation arteries.

multiple nuclei model: a model of urban development in which similar industries locate near one another and shape the characteristics of the immediate neighborhood.

The Nature of Urban Life

gemeinschaft: a type of living situation in which relationships are intimate, cooperative, and personal.

gesellschaft: a type of living situation in which relationships are impersonal and independent.

collective conscience: according to Durkheim, a society's system of fundamental beliefs and values.

social solidarity: according to Durkheim, a product of people's commitment and conformity to the collective conscience.

mechanically integrated society: a situation in which a society's collective conscience is strong and there is a great commitment to that collective conscience.

organically integrated society: a situation in which social solidarity depends on the cooperation of individuals in many different positions who perform specialized tasks.

gentrification: the process by which middle- and upper-class people upgrade marginal areas by displacing the poor.

skid row: an area of the city that has traditionally provided shelter and a degree of tolerance for deviant individuals and activities.

Future Urban Growth in the United States

suburbs: those territories that are part of the metropolitan area but outside the central city.

exurbs: middle and upper-middle class semirural communities located beyond the old suburbs.

KEY THINKERS/RESEARCHERS

Gideon Sjoberg: analyst of the preindustrial city.

U.S. Bureau of the Census: developed a set of terms to describe and classify urban environments.

Robert Park and Ernest Burgess: pioneers in human ecology; developed the concentric zone model of urban development.

Homer Hoyt: developed the sector model of urban development..

C.D. Harris and E.L. Ullman developed the multiple nuclei model of urban development..

Ferdinand Tönnies: developed the concepts of *gemeinschaft* and *gesellschaft* to explain the rural to urban transition.

Émile Durkheim: developed the concept of the collective conscience and mechanical and organic integration as forms of identification with it.

Louis Wirth: proposed a widely accepted definition of the city as a "relatively large, dense, and permanent settlement of socially heterogeneous individuals."

Herbert Gans: helped refocus the way sociologists see urban life by showing that urban residents can and do participate in strong and vital community cultures.

Gerald Suttles: showed that even in poor neighborhoods, people can have a vital culture with norms and values well adapted to the poverty in which the residents live; also that people draw mental maps of the city's neighborhoods.

Georg Simmel: argued that rural social relationships are rich because they encompass a number of role relationships at once, whereas urban relationships tend to be confined to one role set at a time.

Jane Jacobs: argued that social control of public behavior and the patterning of the social interactions of community life take place on the level of blocks rather than entire neighborhoods.

LECTURE SUGGESTIONS

1. **Cities and Civilization.** In the text, Tischler notes that cities are connected to the rise of civilization. Ask students to elaborate on this connection. Historically, why were cities necessary for the development of civilization? What functions did they serve? What resources did they provide which weren't provided elsewhere? Could there be a "civilized" society without cities? Why or why not?

2. **Historical Development of Cities.** From the available evidence, it appears that cities developed at different times in different parts of the world. Ask the students to develop some hypotheses to explain this.

3. **Preindustrial vs. Industrial Cities.** Kirkpatrick Sale, in his book *Human Scale* (see Resources), argues that there is a certain "natural" scale that fits with the physical and social characteristics and abilities of humans. Exceeding the limit creates dysfunction for individuals and the society. In his book, Sale finds numerous examples of humans in preindustrial times living within their physical and social limits in the construction of cities. Indeed, a certain reasonable size and scale seem to be the rule throughout nearly all preindustrial societies, regardless of cultural variation. Not so in the industrial city characterized by ever-increasing gigantism and sprawl. Recount Sale's argument and some of his examples, then have students work on coming up with a list of features of the modern industrial city that out of proportion, either physically or socially, to humans. How shall we rectify these dysfunctions and disorientation?

4. **The Structure of Cities.** All three models of urban structure demonstrate, at a gross level, the operation of market factors. But there are other socioeconomic forces that influence both the market and city structure. These other factors include unequal access to wealth and power, which allows some people and organizations to manipulate the market to their own ends. Rarely do these ends include the maintenance of genuine local community life. A good accessible background source for lectures on this subject is Logan and Molotch (see Resources section).

5. **The Nature of Urban Life.** One feature of urban life that has drawn increasing attention from sociologists is the search for urban community (*gemeinschaft*). Ray Oldenburg's argues in his book, *The Great Good Place* (see Resources), that viable urban communities have always had "third places" between home and work that allow for informal communal socializing. If you present Oldenburg's argument to the class, you should have no trouble generating class discussion about current or remembered "great good places."

6. **William H. Whyte on the City Center.** Whyte's work on what makes "people spaces" in crowded city centers "work" deserves a wider audience. What he says seems like common sense when you hear or read it, yet it goes against most of the urban planning and building that is going on in downtowns across America today. Whyte's book (cited in the box "Sociology at Work") is extensive but easy to access and excerpt. While the box gives students a short summary of the argument, it is worth going further with it. A video is also available, "The Social Life of Small Urban Spaces," that graphically demonstrates Whyte's arguments using New York City as a model. This is such a practical issue, but one where informed citizens really can have an effect on the quality of urban life.

7. **The Global System of Cities.** With the development of an increasingly global economy, civilization and cities have become global as well. Certain cities are "world cities" — the nerve centers of the global economy. But nearly every city nearly everywhere is tied into this network. A good, accessible resource on this subject is Saskia Sassen's *Cities in a World Economy* (see Resources).

SUGGESTED ACTIVITIES

1. **The Preindustrial City.** To exercise their sociological imaginations, have students write a narrative diary of a "day in the life" of an imaginary person or persons in a preindustrial city. The narrative need only be based on Table 16-1 and the supporting material in the text.

2. **Classification of Urban Environments.** Have students classify, according to categories mentioned in the text, the type of settlement where your college or university is located. Then have them classify their hometowns, and share among themselves the relative advantages and disadvantages of different types of urban (or nonurban) environments.

3. **U.S. Metropolitan Areas.** Have students study the data in Table 16-3 on the 15 largest cities in the United States. How might they explain the changes in rank that occurred between 1980 and 1992? What social factors underlie these changes?

4. **Urban Environments.** Construct a chart for comparing the advantages and disadvantages of residing in a small town, a metropolitan statistical area (MSA), or a consolidated metropolitan statistical area (CMSA). Leave the cells blank and let the students fill them in as a result of discussing these issues in small groups.

5. **The Structure of Cities.** Assign students, working in teams, to research your local or a nearby city to determine which model of urban structure it most closely resembles. This assignment can be completed by driving/biking/busing through the city, and/or it can be handled through research at the city's planning and zoning departments and the local chamber of commerce or economic development authority. Make sure that students explain why they think the city is structured the way it is.

6. **Neighborhoods.** Ask students to draw cognitive maps of the place where they grew up and then analyze them in small groups. What types of features stand out? How did they define their local neighborhood? How were its boundaries determined? How significant was their identification with that neighborhood?

7. **Characteristics of the "Good Community."** In a classic article, Roland Warren examined nine variables crucial to community life (e.g., degrees of autonomy, heterogeneity, commitment, and extent of conflict to be tolerated). You might want to create an overhead or a handout that you use as a writing and/or discussion assignment. Ask students to fill in the answers that correspond to their own ideal vision. As a further exercise, you may want to ask them to look for the ideological and/or theoretical perspective that underlies their vision.

8. **Homelessness.** Invite local homeless people (there are bound to be some) and/or their advocates in to discuss the plight of the homeless locally. It is important to try to make this problem less abstract to students. Alternatively, you may want to assign students, after appropriate preparation, to look for homeless people in your community and to discuss their search and its outcome in class.

9. **Suburbs.** Divide the class into those who grew up or now live in suburbs and those who do not now live or did not grow up in suburbs. Have each group discuss among themselves and come up with what they

think are commonly-accepted stereotypes of the other group. Then have them share these stereotypes with the other group and discuss them.

10. **SimCity: An Urban Policy Simulation.** This highly-regarded computer simulation allows the user to make crucial economic, political, and social policy decisions and to see the results of those decisions. Demonstrates very well the interrelatedness of issues and the problem of unintended consequences. Available for Macintosh, DOS, or Windows, a special version is available as an ancillary from Harcourt Brace. Talk to your sales representative.

RESOURCES FOR STUDENTS

The Development of Cities

Janet L. Abu-Lughod, *Changing Cities: Urban Sociology.* New York: HarperCollins, 1991.
> A comprehensive, introduction to urban sociology, from the earliest cities to contemporary urban issues.

Saskia Sassen, *Cities in a World Economy.* Thousand Oaks, CA: Pine Forge Press, 1994.
> An excellent introduction to the changing role and structure of cities in the global economy. For a short paperback, it is surprisingly comprehensive.

Urbanization

John R.Logan and Harvey L. Molotch, *Urban Fortunes: The Political Economy of Place.* Berkeley: University of California Press, 1987.
> Traces the development and current problems of capitalist cities in terms of local conflicts over growth.

The Nature of Urban Life

Bill Berkowitz, *Community Dreams: Ideas for Enriching Neighborhood and Community Life.* San Luis Obispo, CA: Impact Publishers, 1984.
> A uniquely offbeat compilation of practical and far-out ideas for enriching neighborhood and community life from a veteran grass-roots community organizer.

Ray Oldenburg, *The Great Good Place: Cafés, Coffee Shops, Community Centers, Beauty Parlors, General Stores, Bars, Hangouts and How They Get You Through the Day.* New York: Paragon House, 1989.
> A unique look at what the author calls "third places" between home and work that allow for informal, communal socializing and which are the real foundations, he argues, for a viable community life.

Future Urban Growth in the United States

Mark Baldassare, *Trouble in Paradise: The Suburban Transformation in America.* New York: Columbia University Press, 1986.
> Looks at current challenges facing suburbia and why many suburbanites have soured on their would-be utopias.

Kirkpatrick Sale, *Human Scale, 2nd edition.* New York: G.P. Putnam, 1982.
> A provocative book in which the author argues that for most of human history we have lived on a humanly-manageable scale. Only recently have our cities, our architecture, and our institutions become overwhelmingly large — too large to comprehend and deal with. The solution he proposes is a return to truly human scale.

CHAPTER SEVENTEEN: Health and Health Care

CHAPTER OUTLINE

The Experience of Illness

Health Care in the United States
    Gender and Health
    Sociology at Work: Women, Men and the Caretaker Role
    Race and Health
    Social Class and Health
    Age and Health
    Women in Medicine

Contemporary Health-Care Issues
    Acquired Immunodeficiency Syndrome (AIDS)
    Health Insurance
    Taking the Sociological Perspective: Do We Focus on Sick Care Instead of Health Care?
    Preventing Illness

World Health Trends
    The Health of Infants and Children in Developing Countries
        Child Killers
        Maternal Health
        Maternal Age
        Maternal Education
        Breast-feeding
    Controversies in Sociology: Is Disease Caused by Our State of Mind?

LEARNING OBJECTIVES

1. Describe the basic elements of the sick role.

2. Describe the basic characteristics of the U.S. health-care system.

3. Explain the link between basic demographic factors and health.

4. Describe the nature and extent of the AIDS crisis.

5. Compare and contrast the three major models of illness prevention.

6. Describe the factors involved in the health of infants and children in developing countries.

KEY CONCEPTS

The Experience of Illness
> *sick role:* a shared set of cultural norms that legitimates deviant behavior caused by illness and channels the individual into the health-care system.

Contemporary Health-Care Issues
> *acquired immunodeficiency syndrome (AIDS):* a specific group of diseases or conditions that indicate severe immunosuppression related to infection with the human immunodeficiency virus.

> *third-party payments:* a system in which the costs of an individual's health care are paid for by some form of public or private insurance or charitable organization.

> *fee-for-service system:* a system by which doctors are paid only for treating illness.

World Health Trends
> *health:* a state of complete mental, physical, and social well-being.

KEY THINKERS/RESEARCHERS

Talcott Parsons: American sociologist who developed the concept of the sick role.

Centers for Disease Control (CDC): a part of the U.S. Public Health Service, this agency is charged with monitoring communicable ailments.

World Health Organization (WHO): an international organization that monitors health issues.

Blair Justice: argues that disease is mostly a result of a failure of our personal social psychological coping mechanisms.

Arthur Frank: argues that personality theories of disease engage in blaming the victim, but persist because there is a payoff for everyone involved.

LECTURE SUGGESTIONS

1. **Health Care in the United States.** Tischler makes the point that, "even with our large investment in health care, Americans are not the healthiest people in the world." Reinforce this point by bringing to class comparative health statistics from other countries around the world such as those cumulated and published by the Population Reference Bureau (citation in the Chapter 15 Resources section). There are figures here that many students will find surprising. In discussing the figures, it is important to try to wean students away from the view that health and health care are about technology, when in fact comparative data show us that health is more influenced by sociocultural factors.

2. **The Debate over Health Care in the United States.** Health care is clearly one of the "hot" issues of the 90s. At least every week, there is news of some major initiative or policy change in the private or public sector. If you pay attention to the popular media, you can cull stories on developments and perspectives, pro and con, as you go so that when you get to this part of the class you can jog students' memories and have them debate these pros and cons.

3. **Social Class and Health.** Tischler observes that "studies of life expectancy show that on every measure, social class influences longevity." In light of this, isn't the most effective strategy for improving and guaranteeing the health of the population to eradicate poverty and reduce or eliminate social class inequalities? Pose this question to the class. If you have a free or low-income health clinic in your community or nearby, try to get someone to come in to class and talk about the type and volume of both health and social problems they see.

4. **AIDS.** Have a PWA (person with AIDS) and/or someone from a local AIDS task force come in to class to discuss their experiences, particularly with prejudice and discrimination against them. An excellent video for showing the human impact of the AIDS epidemic is "Common Threads," a documentary about some of the people represented in the AIDS Quilt and the loved ones who labored to remember the victim by crafting a uniquely expressive panel. This is a very moving video; it really personalizes the issues in a way that makes it hard for students to dismiss. To illustrate the importance of social interaction and support to health, put on reserve or bring into class Sal Lopes's beautifully-photographed book *Living With AIDS* (see Resources). It includes photos and diaries of AIDS "buddies" who help AIDS victims live and die with dignity.

5. **Health Insurance.** Set up a panel with someone from the health insurance industry, a physician in private practice, and someone who administers Medicaid payments to discuss various problems in this area. Have students be prepared to focus on possible sociological explanations for these problems.

6. **The Health of Infants and Children in Developing Countries.** Ask students to pretend that they have been hired as consultants to a developing country on how to reduce the number of child deaths. Collectively work through the development of each recommendation, based on material in the text. Ask students how they would try to implement these recommendations, and who might oppose them.

SUGGESTED ACTIVITIES

1. **The Experience of Illness.** In small groups, have students discuss the sick role along the lines suggested in the learning objective exercise in the Study Guide. You might want to have them focus on deviance from the socially-sanctioned sick role, and how we deal with that deviance.

2. **Gender and Health.** In the text Tischler says, "While men have shorter life expectancies, women appear to be sick more often." Divide the class by sex (this is, probably, one of the few times it is appropriate) and have each group discuss among themselves examples and explanations of the characteristics of the *other* sex. When each group has drawn up a list, bring them together (but keep it civil!) to discuss stereotypes, biases, and, possibly, biological truths.

3. **Race, Gender, and Health.** Have students examine Table 17-2 in the text and then, in small groups, try to work out sociological explanations for 1) the relative position of the four groups, and 2) the changes that have occurred in life expectancy from 1900 to 1989.

4. **AIDS.** Ask students to discuss the extent to which AIDS has affected their lifestyle. You may want to do an anonymous questionnaire asking about safe sex, number of partners, avoidance of sex, avoidance of relationships that might lead to sex, etc.

5. **Preventing Illness.** Using Table 17-3 and the supporting exposition as a guide, have students attempt to apply these three models by developing three sets of social policies with regard to specific illnesses — e.g., drug abuse (mentioned in the Study Guide), AIDS, heart disease, etc. After they have developed the

policies ask students to reflect on the social implications of carrying out each perspective's policies.

6. **Health.** Have students read the definition of health in the text and then try to think of ways it could be measured. Remind them not to restrict themselves to quantitative measures, but to think about qualitative and unobtrusive measures as well.

RESOURCES FOR STUDENTS

The Experience of Illness
Rachel Spector, *Cultural Diversity in Health and Illness, 2nd edition.* Norwalk, CN: Appleton-Century-Crofts, 1985.
  An exploration of the role played by race, ethnicity and other cultural factors in health and illness.

Contemporary Health Care Issues in the United States
Victor Gong, M.D. and Norman Rudnick, eds., *AIDS: Facts and Issues.* New Brunswick, NJ: Rutgers University Press, 1986.
  One of the best handbooks about AIDS. It has extensive, easily-accessible discussions of medical, legal, ethical, social, political, and spiritual issues associated with AIDS. An extensive list of resources is included.

Sal Lopes, *Living With AIDS: A Photographic Journal.* Boston: Bullfinch Press, 1994.
  A moving photographic look at 3 aspects of AIDS: The Quilt, a selection of partners in a Buddy program, and a family that adopts an infant with AIDS. Lopes exhibits a great deal of sensitivity towards his subjects. Includes excerpts from the subjects' Buddy journals.

Randy Shilts, *And the Band Played On: Politics, People, and the AIDS Epidemic.* New York: St. Martin's Press, 1987.
  A critical examination of the official neglect of the AIDS epidemic by the medical and political establishments as long as the primary victims seemed to be members of deviant subcultures.

Paul Starr, *The Transformation of American Medicine.* New York: Basic Books, 1982.
  An award-winning analysis of the development of the medical profession and the contemporary implications of its control over the delivery of health care.

Bonnie Szumski, *The Health Crisis: Opposing Viewpoints.* San Diego: Greenhaven Press, 1989.
  A debate on contemporary health care issues.

World Health Trends
Vicente Navarro, *Imperialism, Health and Medicine.* Farmingdale, NY: Baywood Publishing, 1981.
  An argument that socioeconomic factors play the greatest role in determining the health of people in the Third World by a physician who is also a sociologist.

David R. Phillips, *Health and Health Care in the Third World.* New York: Wiley, 1990.
  An examination of the basic health issues confronting Third World countries.

CHAPTER EIGHTEEN: Collective Behavior and Social Movements

CHAPTER OUTLINE

Theories of Collective Behavior
  Contagion ("Mentalist") Theory
  Emergent Norm Theory
  Convergence Theory
  Value-Added Theory

Crowds: Concentrated Collectivities
  Attributes of Crowds
  Types of Crowds
    Acting Crowd
    Threatened Crowd
    Expressive Crowd
    Conventional Crowd
    Casual Crowd
  The Changeable Nature of Crowds

Dispersed Collective Behavior
  Fads and Fashions
  Rumors
  Public Opinion
  Mass Hysteria and Panic

Social Movements
  Relative Deprivation Theory
  Resource Mobilization Theory
  Types of Social Movements
    Reactionary Social Movement
    Conservative Social Movement
    Revisionary Social Movement
    Revolutionary Social Movement
    Expressive Social Movement
  Taking the Sociological Perspective: Do Men's Groups Constitute a Social Movement?
  The Life Cycle of Social Movements
    Incipiency
    Coalescence

Institutionalization

Fragmentation

Demise

LEARNING OBJECTIVES

1. Contrast theories of collective behavior.

2. Describe the attributes and types of crowds.

3. Describe dispersed forms of collective behavior.

4. Contrast alternative theories of social movements.

5. Describe the major types of social movements.

6. Describe the life cycle of social movements.

KEY CONCEPTS

Theories of Collective Behavior

collective behavior: relatively spontaneous social actions that occur when people respond to unstructured and ambiguous situations.

contagion theory: the theory that crowd behavior is caused by a kind of irrational group feeling that spreads among individuals, causing them to lose their inhibitions and become more receptive to group sentiments.

emergent norm theory: a theory that crowd members develop common standards by observing and listening to one another.

convergence theory: a theory that collective behavior is the result of people with similar characteristics being drawn together.

value-added theory: a theory that collective behavior occurs as a result of six necessary social conditions or processes that build on one another.

structural conduciveness: a condition in the existing social order that may promote collective behavior.

structural strain: a condition in which a group's ideals conflict with its everyday realities.

Crowds: Concentrated Collectivities

crowd: a temporary concentration of people who focus on some thing or event but who also are attuned to one another's behavior.

acting crowd: a group of people whose passions and tempers have been aroused by some focal event, who come to share a purpose, and who feed off one another's arousal, often erupting into spontaneous acts of violence.

threatened crowd: a crowd that is in a state of alarm, believing some kind of danger is present.

expressive crowd: a group of people drawn together by the promise of personal gratification through active participation in activities and events.

conventional crowd: a gathering in which people's behavior conforms to some well-established set of cultural norms, and gratification results from passive appreciation of an event.

casual crowd: any collection of people who just happen, in the course of their private activities, to be in one place at the same time and focus their attention on a common object or event.

Dispersed Collective Behavior

mass: a collection of people who, although physically dispersed, participate in some event either physically or with a common concern or interest.

fad: a social change with a very short life span marked by a rapid spread and an abrupt drop in popularity.

craze: a fad that is especially short-lived.

fashion: the standards of dress or manners in a given society at a certain time.

rumor: information that is shared informally and spreads quickly through a mass or crowd.

public opinion: beliefs held by a dispersed collectivity of individuals about a common problem, interest, focus, or activity.

propaganda: advertisements of a political nature, seeking to mobilize public support behind one specific party, candidate, or point of view.

opinion leaders: socially acknowledged experts to whom the public turns for advice.

mass hysteria: a condition in which large numbers of people are overwhelmed with emotion and frenzied activity or become convinced that they have experienced something for which investigators can find no discernible evidence.

panic: an uncoordinated group flight from a perceived danger.

Social Movements

social movement: a form of collective behavior in which large numbers of people are organized or alerted to support and bring about, or to resist, social change.

relative deprivation theory: suggests that social movements occur when large numbers of people experience the feeling that they lack the living or working conditions, political rights, or social dignity to which they are entitled.

resource mobilization theory: argues that social movements arise at certain times because skilled leaders know how to mobilize and channel popular discontent.

reactionary social movement: movements that embrace the aims of the past and seek to return the general society to yesterday's values.

conservative social movement: movements that seek to maintain society's current values by reacting to change or threats of change they believe will undermine the status quo.

revisionary social movement: movements that seek partial or slight changes within the existing order but do not threaten the order itself.

revolutionary social movement: movements that seek to overthrow all or nearly all of the existing social order and replace it with an order they consider more suitable.

expressive social movement: movements that stress personal feelings of satisfaction or well-being and typically arise to fill some void or to distract people from some great dissatisfaction in their lives.

incipiency: the beginning stage of a social movement.

coalescence: the stage of a social movement when groups form around leaders, begin to promote policies, and promulgate programs.

institutionalization: the stage of a social movement when it becomes firmly established through formal organizations.

fragmentation: the state of a social movement when the movement begins to fall apart.

demise: refers to the end of a social movement.

KEY THINKERS/RESEARCHERS

Gustave Le Bon: French sociologist who was a pioneer in the study of collective behavior and who developed the contagion theory of crowds.

Herbert Blumer: a major figure in the study of social movements; discussed contagion theory, classified types of crowds, and first discussed expressive social movements.

Ralph H. Turner: one of the first sociologists to develop the emergent norm theory of collective behavior.

Neil Smelser: developed the value-added theory of collective behavior.

Elias Canetti: described the important traits of crowds.

Alfred A. Kroeber: showed that fashion moves through predictable cycles correlated with degrees of political and social stability.

Georg Simmel: argued that changes in fashion are adopted by the upper class as a way of keeping themselves distinct from the lower classes.

Irving Janis: described the conditions under which people collectively panic.

Kai Erikson: explained the seventeenth-century Salem witchcraft trials as an episode of mass hysteria created by the Massachusetts Bay Colony's identity crisis.

Samuel Stouffer: first described the concept of relative deprivation.

Saul Alinsky: a renowned activist leader who was especially good at mobilizing community resources into social movements.

William Bruce Cameron: classified social movements into four basic types.

Armand L. Mauss: suggested that social movements typically pass through a series of stages that are the equivalent of a biological life cycle.

LECTURE SUGGESTIONS

1. **The Nature of Collective Behavior.** Tischler suggests in this chapter that there are two ways of viewing collective behavior: as functional or as pathological. Ask the class if it is possible to view collective behavior as *neither* positive or negative — i.e., as something that just occurs among social animals like humans. Examine the implications of holding each of these understandings of collective behavior.

2. **Theories of Collective Behavior.** After describing the contagion, emergent norm, and convergence theories of collective behavior Tischler points out some problems with each theory. Based on these negative statements, see if you can, working collectively with the class, describe the positive criteria for an adequate theory of collective behavior. That is, what are the key things that it would have to explain? How could this theory be tested? Write these criteria on the board or an overhead. This is a good exercise in critical thinking and social theorizing.

3. **Value-Added Theory and the Life-Cycle of Social Movements.** In the Resources section of this chapter is a handout I developed to explain Smelser's theory to students and to help them see how it operates over the life cycle of a social movement. You will note some modifications that I have added: 1) stressing the importance of *internal*, as well as external, mechanisms of social control, particularly the sticky issue of who is part of the movement and who isn't; 2) in the life cycle, stressing that fragmentation and demise can come about as a result of *success* as well as failure. Otherwise students are left with too cynical an interpretation of the possibilities of social movements. While it is of course a matter of perspective, one could certainly say that, on their own terms, movements like the abolitionist, woman's suffrage, civil rights, and anti-Vietnam War movements were very successful. See if your students can use the categories on this handout to analyze a social movement. You could help them by showing one of the many film or video documentary histories of movements.

4. **Fashion and Social Class.** Tischler suggests that Simmel's argument that fashion is a tool of the upper class to try to keep itself distinct may no longer be true today. See if students can think of examples that support Simmel's argument as well as ones that contradict it. What is their assessment?

5. **Mass Hysteria and Group Solidarity.** Tischler mentions Kai Erikson's famous sociological analysis of the Salem witchcraft trials. You may want to share more details of this classic study with your class, as it is an excellent example of how sociology can rationally explain phenomena that many people view as fundamentally irrational and inexplicable.

6. **Theories of Collective Behavior and Social Movements.** Earlier in this chapter students learned that Smelser's value-added theory of collective behavior is one of the best theories in this area. Which of the two theories of social movements mentioned here — relative deprivation or resource-mobilization theory — best fits with Smelser's scheme? Why?

SUGGESTED ACTIVITIES

1. **Crowds and Theories of Collective Behavior.** If possible, assign students to do participant observation in a crowd situation. (Something should be going on near you — a concert, sporting event, political rally, etc.) On the basis of their observations, have them classify the crowd by type and then to write about and

discuss in class the theory of collective behavior that best seems to explain what they observed.

2. **Fads and Fashions.** Have students perform a content analysis of the fads and fashions of an earlier time. They could use books, popular magazines, hit records, films, etc. What cultural messages were transmitted by the artifacts and practices of the time? After completing this exercise, have students analyze contemporary society. What are today's fads and fashions all about?

3. **Rumors.** You can demonstrate to the class how rumors become exaggerated and distorted by writing down a rumor that may appeal to the students in your class, having one student read it silently, and then whisper it to the student next to them, who passes it on to the next student, and so on, around the room. When it gets to the last student, have them repeat the rumor aloud to the class. Then read the original aloud. How did the rumor get distorted? What are the implications of the particular distortions it underwent?

4. **Types of Social Movements.** After discussing the general categories of social movements, have students generate a list of contemporary movements and attempt to classify them. You may want to be prepared with examples of movements that are not easily classified as one type, so that students really have to think through the criteria. How important are these criteria, and how useful is this classification scheme?

RESOURCES FOR STUDENTS

Crowds: Concentrated Collectivities

Hugh Davis Graham and Ted Robert Gurr, eds., *Violence in America: Historical and Comparative Perspectives, revised edition.* Beverly Hills, CA: Sage Publications, 1979.
>   An excellent history of violence connected with crowds and social movements, it also examines violence perpetrated by the state.

Dispersed Collective Behavior

Stuart Ewen, *Captains of Consciousness: Advertising and the Social Roots of the Consumer Culture.* New York: McGraw-Hill, 1976.
>   Argues that capitalists, using advertising as propaganda, were able to reshape popular culture into a consumer culture in this century.

Edward S. Herman, *Beyond Hypocrisy: Decoding the News in an Age of Propaganda.* Boston: South End Press, 1992.
>   An irreverent book that includes satirical essays, cartoons, and a cross-referenced lexicon of government doublespeak terminology with examples.

Social Movements

Todd Gitlin, *The Sixties: Years of Hope, Days of Rage.* New York: Bantam, 1987.
>   The author of this highly-acclaimed book was a national leader of the student movement in the 1960s who later became a respected sociologist. This book provides his sociological reflections and insights into the movement and the period.

Frances Fox Piven and Richard A. Cloward, *Poor People's Movements: Why They Succeed, How They Fail.* New York: Vintage, 1979.
>   An analysis of four different social movements involving poor people, the book suggests strategies aimed at maximizing gains for the poor.

SOCIAL CONDITIONS THAT PROMOTE COLLECTIVE BEHAVIOR/SOCIAL MOVEMENTS

Each of these is a necessary, but not sufficient condition to promote collective behavior. Moreover, the conditions exist in a hierarchy, such that earlier conditions must be met before later ones can occur.

1. Structural Conduciveness
- objective conditions in the social structure that promote or discourage collective action
- i.e., in order to generate collective action, there must be something objectively wrong

2. Structural Strain
- tension between group ideals a social reality
- a social definition that something is wrong

3. Growth and Spread of a Generalized Belief
- shared popular explanations of what the problem is
- competing explanations create ambiguity and lead to more unstructured collective behavior

4. Precipitating Factors
- an event or series of events that triggers a collective response ("the last straw")
- difficult to predict or create

5. Mobilization for Action
- organized, patterned social interaction
- may be formal or informal

6. Mechanisms of Social Control
- internal: solutions to organizational dilemmas such as mechanisms of communication, decisionmaking, handling deviance, etc.
- external: institutional response to the perceived threat of collective action
    options: repression, cooptation, concessions

THE LIFE-CYCLE OF SOCIAL MOVEMENTS

1. Incipiency
- period when the movement begins
- encompasses conditions 1 – 4 above; movement won't begin until all are satisfied

2. Coalescence
- the movement comes together and begins to get organized
- encompasses conditions 5 and 6 above

3. Institutionalization
- movement becomes firmly established
- continues conditions 5 and 6 above

4. Fragmentation
- movement begins to break up
- negative aspect: due to internal problems and/or external mechanisms of social control
- positive aspect: represents greater sophistication and a division of labor in solving the problem

5. Demise
- the movement ends
- due to either success or institutional response that destroys it

162

CHAPTER NINETEEN: Social Change

CHAPTER OUTLINE

Society and Social Change

Sources of Social Change

Internal Sources of Social Change

Technological Innovation

Ideology

Reactions to Institutionalized Inequality

External Sources of Social Change

Theories of Social Change

Evolutionary Theory

Conflict Theory

Functionalist Theory

Cyclical (Rise and Fall) Theory

Sociology at Work: George Ritzer on the McDonaldization of Society

Modernization: Global Social Change

Modernization: An Overview

Modernization in the Third World

Modernization and the Individual

Social Change in the United States

Technological Change

Controversies in Sociology: Are We Too Willing to Embrace the Information Highway?

The Workforce of the Future

LEARNING OBJECTIVES

1. Describe the nature of social change in society.

2. Contrast differing ideologies and show how they influence social change.

3. Explain the processes of cultural diffusion and forced acculturation.

4. Compare alternative theories of social change.

5. Describe the characteristics and impact of the process of modernization.

6. Describe the phenomenon of technological innovation.

7.   Summarize the changes that will occur in the U.S. labor force by the year 2000.

KEY CONCEPTS

Society and Social Change

social change: any modification in the social organization of a society in any of its social institutions or social roles.

Sources of Social Change

internal sources of social change: those factors that originate within a specific society and that singly or in combination produce significant alterations in its social organization and structure.

ideology: a set of interrelated religious or secular beliefs, values, and norms that justify the pursuit of a given set of goals through a given set of means.

conservative ideologies: ideologies that try to preserve things as they are.

liberal ideologies: ideologies that seek limited reforms that do not involve fundamental changes in the social structure of society.

radical ideologies: ideologies that seek major structural changes in society.

external sources of social change: changes within a society produced by events outside of it.

forced acculturation: a social change that is imposed by might or conquest on weaker peoples.

Theories of Social Change

evolution: the continuous change from a simpler condition to a more complex state.

homeostatic system: an assemblage of interrelated parts that seeks to achieve and maintain a settled or stable state.

ideational cultures: cultures that emphasize spiritual values.

sensate cultures: cultures that are based on what is immediately apparent through the senses.

idealistic point: the point at which sensate and ideational values coexist in a harmonious mix.

McDonaldization: the idea that the rationalized business principles by which McDonald's is run are coming to dominate modern society.

Modernization: Global Social Change

modernization: a complex set of changes that take place as a traditional society becomes an industrial one.

Social Change in the United States

technological determinism: the view that technology alone is largely responsible for social change.

KEY THINKERS/RESEARCHERS

Hans Gerth and C. Wright Mills: developed the definition of social change.

Edward Shils: developed the concept of mass society.

Lauriston Sharp: described the disruptive effects of the diffusion of steel axes to the Yir Yoront tribe.

Charles Darwin: the most influential evolutionary theorist, he systematized the concept in his book *On the Origin of Species.*

Herbert Spencer: brought Darwin's idea of natural selection into sociology and suggested that Western cultures had reached higher levels of cultural development because they were better adapted.

Émile Durkheim: a pioneering evolutionary sociologist, he described the transition from mechanical to organic solidarity.

Ferdinand Tönnies: described social evolution as a shift from *gemeinschaft* to *gesellschaft.*

Julian H. Steward: proposed the concept of multilineal evolution as a way of avoiding ethnocentrism in the concept.

Marshall Sahlins and Elman Service: distinguished between the general process of differentiation and the specific evolution of each society.

Karl Marx: a pioneering conflict theorist, he argued that social change is rooted in class conflict.

Ralf Dahrendorf: argued that conflict and dissent are present in nearly every part of society.

Talcott Parsons: the best-known functionalist theorist in America, he saw society as a "homeostatic action system."

William F. Ogburn: developed the concept of cultural lag in an effort to provide a functionalist explanation for disequilibrium.

Oswald Spengler: theorized that every society moves through a life cycle.

Arnold Toynbee: argued that the rise and fall of civilizations could be explained through the concepts of challenge and response.

Pitirim Sorokin: distinguished between ideational and sensate cultures.

George Ritzer: proposed the concept of the "McDonaldization" of society.

Alex Inkeles and David Smith: demonstrated the positive psychological effects of modernization through a cross-cultural study.

Max Weber: felt that the process of modernization through increasing rationality could have a damaging effect on the spirit of individuals.

Colin Turnbull: studied the cultural and social disintegration of the Ik of Uganda as they experienced forced acculturation.

LECTURE SUGGESTIONS

1. **Cultural Diffusion.** What are the implications of the diffusion of American culture worldwide? You might want to bring in some recent examples of controversies abroad — e.g., demonstrations against EuroDisney, McDonald's on the Champs Elysées, etc. What are the positive and negative functions of this? But it is not just a one-way street. Ask students to think about what aspects of other cultures have diffused into American culture. Possible categories include food (tacos, pizza, pita), music (west African rhythms in jazz, pop, and rock), and language (Native American place names).

2. **Forced Acculturation.** The treatment of Native Americans affords many examples of this process. One particularly good video portraying Native American children being forced to learn English and dress like Europeans is *Where the Spirit Lives.*

3. **Cultural Lag.** Ask students for examples of cultural lag in American society today. For example, computers are appearing everywhere and for nearly every purpose, but many people still have "computerphobia." Or: Why haven't we gone to a "cashless" economy, and why do people insist on keeping pennies in circulation? What about the movement of large numbers of women into the labor force, but the persistence of old stereotypes about women workers, sexual harassment, and perceptions of parenting?

4. **The McDonaldization of Society.** Ritzer's concept is provocative, and one that many students will be able to relate to. Ask students who have worked in the fast food industry to share some of their experiences with the class. Ask students who have had jobs in other areas that have "McDonaldized" to share those experiences. You may want to present some other examples to the class. An excellent source for those examples is Garson's *The Electronic Sweatshop* (see Resources).

5. **Modernization.** Many people in industrial society tend to think of modernization as a unilinear process that always (despite occasionally heavy costs) results in progress. To get a perspective on this, invite an anthropologist into class to discuss so-called "primitive" societies. Is it appropriate to call their technology "primitive" — e.g., how many of us could successfully gather our subsistence with just a "simple" digging stick? What about the fact that we seem to work much harder and longer than people in hunting and gathering societies, and with less apparent satisfaction? Students will undoubtedly reply, "But look at all the wonderful stuff we have in modern society!" True, but is it progress? Does it bring more happiness? By providing this background and raising these questions you will be getting students to think critically about the tradeoffs involved in making social changes to become more "modern."

6. **Technological Change: The Internet.** The Internet began as a way for scientists and academics to communicate quickly and efficiently with one another. In the last several years, however, it has grown exponentially, but in a haphazard, grass-roots, democratic, and unregulated way. Now, various groups are calling for regulation of the Internet. Some groups do not want children to have access to images they consider pornographic. Financial institutions are wary about conducting business over the Internet, they say, without some reliable centralized control. This raises the question of control of technology. Ask students what they think. Do we need centralized control and regulation of technology? Is it possible to have a democratic technology? What are the implications? You might direct students to think about the automobile as a parallel.

7. **The Workforce of the Future.** Conduct an anonymous survey of students on their projected occupation after graduation. Compile the results and compare them with Figures 19-1 and 19-2. Ask students to describe the factors that went into their career choice. For instance, to what extent were they influenced by occupational projections such as what appears in the text? What other considerations were/are

important? This may be a good place for you to highlight the point made by Tischler, that education is closely related to occupational projections. Congratulate students for being in college, but urge them to get a substantive education and not just accumulate credits. The credential purchased with the credits will be important in getting them in the door, but students' future success on the job will depend on the quality of their knowledge and skills. Urge them not to shortchange themselves.

SUGGESTED ACTIVITIES

1. **Society and Social Change.** In small groups, have students generate a list of the five major social changes that they think have taken place so far during their lifetimes. Then ask them to project into the future: What are the five most important social changes that they think are likely to occur over the next 20 years? How will our society be different because of these changes?

2. **Competing Ideologies.** There are a number of good books and readers that take a sociological perspective on competing ideologies. One that I use is Gary Alan Fine's *Talking Sociology* (citation in sample syllabus in the Appendix to the Introduction of this manual). Fine's book is relatively short, easily accessible to students, and , most of all, shows them the importance of understanding ideologies and ideological agendas in society.

3. **Theories of Social Change.** Develop a handout that lists the theories of social change discussed in the text. Ask students to write in the strengths and weaknesses of each theory, and what it seems to explain best, and what it has the hardest time explaining.

4. **Ideational vs. Sensate Culture.** Have students discuss which kind of culture the United States currently has. Has it always been so? Can students think of a time when the opposite model prevailed? Have we as a society ever been at the idealistic point, as described by Sorokin?

5. **Assessing Technological Change.** In the Resources section at the end of this chapter is a set of guidelines for assessing technology. Divide students into groups, have them choose a technology and then assess and make recommendations regarding that technology according to the guidelines. In the presentation/discussion phase in class, ask students to reflect on how many decisions about technology are made all the time, without benefit of this socially-conscious process, and certainly without their input. Does knowing this, and now understanding the guidelines create "information anxiety" for them?

6. **Information Anxiety.** Ask students to recount their own personal experiences with information anxiety. There are really two dimensions to this: too much information, and access to information out of our control. Example of the first phenomenon: doing a computerized bibliographical or book search in the library and getting more references than you could wade through in a lifetime. Example of the second phenomenon: having some computer operator somewhere make an error and soundly screw up your financial life.

RESOURCES FOR STUDENTS

Sources of Social Change
Thomas S. Kuhn, *The Structure of Scientific Revolutions, 2nd edition, enlarged.* Chicago: University of Chicago Press, 1970.
> A classic work on the role of conflict and consensus in advancing scientific thought.

Modernization: Global Social Change
Thomas Richard Shannon, *An Introduction to the World-System Perspective.* Boulder, CO: Westview Press, 1989.
> An accessible introduction to one of the most important theories on global change and development. Includes history, basic concepts, critique, and assessment.

Social Change in the United States
Barbara Garson, *The Electronic Sweatshop: How Computers Are Transforming the Office of the Future Into the Factory of the Past.* New York: Penguin, 1988.
> Incorporates oral history with insightful analysis of technological change in white-collar and service industry jobs.

Bennett Harrison and Barry Bluestone, *The Great U-Turn: Corporate Restructuring and the Polarizing of America.* New York: Basic Books, 1988.
> Two important analysts of the changing American economy examine the social consequences of current economic policies.

David F. Noble, *Forces of Production: A Social History of Industrial Automation.* New York: Oxford University Press, 1986.
> An excellent critical history of how technology has been used — and misused — in the workplace.

GUIDELINES FOR THE ASSESSMENT OF TECHNOLOGY

Technical description
- What is the technology?
- How does it work?
- Who developed this technology?
- Why? What problem was this technology developed to solve?
- How do the above two factors shape its development and alter its possible applications?

Impact assessment

values
- What values underlie your assessment?

society and the environment
- How does this technology alter the relationship of humans to nature?

institutions
- How does this technology affect existing institutional arrangements?

social groups
- How does this technology alter the way humans relate to and with one another?
- What social groups stand to gain the most from this technology?
- What social groups stand to gain the least?

individuals
- Does this technology enhance human creative capacities or limit and inhibit them? How? In what ways?
- Does this technology enable people to better understand the circumstances of their lives, or does it mystify them?
- How is the introduction/proliferation of this technology likely to affect individual self-determination, freedom, and self-esteem?
- Would the introduction/proliferation of this technology enhance or restrict democratic participation in society? How?

Implementation
- What are the key variables affecting implementation?
  — it is more effective to focus on malleable variables (i.e., ones that can be altered)
    symbolic phenomena, rather than natural resources, are easier to change
    continuous, rather than dichotomous variables are easier to alter
  — it is better to have a relatively specific rather than a broad focus
- What are your major recommendations?
- What are the potential social consequences of these recommendations?
  — intended consequences (manifest functions)
  — unintended consequences (latent functions)
- What is the likelihood that your recommendations will be implemented?
  — identification of stakeholders
  — What resources does each possess?
  — identification of stakeholder positions on the issues
- What are the likely consequences if your recommendations are ignored?